W9-BTL-287

GLENN'S
Auto Troubleshooting Guide

Other Books by Harold T. Glenn

Auto Repair Manual

Automobile Engine Rebuilding and Maintenance

Automobile Power Accessories

Exploring Power Mechanics

Youth at the Wheel

Automechanics

Safe Living

MG, Morris and Magnette Repair and Tune-Up Guide

Foreign Carburetors and Electrical Systems Guide

Austin, Austin-Healey Repair and Tune-Up Guide

Sunbeam-Hillman Repair and Tune-Up Guide

Alfa Romeo Repair and Tune-Up Guide

Volkswagen Repair and Tune-Up Guide

Volkswagen Repair and Tune-Up Guide (Spanish Edition)

Triumph Repair and Tune-Up Guide

Mercedes-Benz Repair and Tune-Up Guide

Peugeot Repair and Tune-Up Guide

Renault Repair and Tune-Up Guide

Jaguar Repair and Tune-Up Guide

Volvo Repair and Tune-Up Guide

Fiat Repair and Tune-Up Guide

Foreign Car Repair Manual

GLENN'S
Auto Troubleshooting Guide

HAROLD T. GLENN

*Member, Society of Automotive
Engineers; Formerly, Instructor in
Long Beach Unified School District,
Long Beach, California*

ILLUSTRATED

CHILTON BOOK COMPANY
Philadelphia   New York   London

Copyright © 1962, 1964, 1966 by
HAROLD T. GLENN

Second Printing, June 1966
Third Printing, February 1967
Fourth Printing, April 1968
Fifth Printing, February 1969
Sixth Printing, August 1969

All Rights Reserved

Published in Philadelphia by Chilton Book Company,
and simultaneously in Ontario, Canada, by Thomas Nelson & Sons, Ltd.

Manufactured in the United States of America
by Quinn & Boden Company, Inc., Rahway, N. J.

Contents

vi   Contents

Troubleshooting

Troubleshooting is done before a unit is disassembled so that the mechanic can give the car owner an estimate of the cost of the repair job. It helps the mechanic to pinpoint the trouble so that he will know what to look for as the unit is being disassembled. Then, too, troubleshooting will frequently cut down on the amount of time spent on repair, provided that the defective section can be pinpointed accurately.

The material in this chapter is organized so as to cover both types of troubleshooting; with and without specialized test equipment. Actually, there is no substitute for accurate equipment. However, there are times when a quick test is needed to localize trouble which saves the time of hooking up a battery of test equipment. Besides the saving of time, developing a familiarity with the various testing possibilities results in a depth of understanding that enables a mechanic to do a better job—and a quicker one, too.

In addition, there are times when a mechanic is called on to locate troubles under somewhat less than ideal conditions. This happens when he is sent to start a car stalled at some distance from the garage. Naturally, he cannot carry all the specialized testing equipment with him. He has to depend on some rather simple tests to locate the trouble in order to start the engine. When the car is brought back to the garage, then he can use his accurate equipment to check further and to make the necessary repairs which caused the original breakdown.

EMERGENCY TROUBLESHOOTING

BASIC STARTING TROUBLE TESTS

When an engine is difficult to start, or does not start at all, it is necessary to use a logical procedure to locate the trouble. Basically, the problem of hard starting can be broken down into four areas of trouble: cranking, ignition, fuel, and compression. The tests are made in that order, as shown on the roadmap.

When the trouble is localized to one of these four areas, the mechanic can then proceed to make one of the more detailed tests described for each

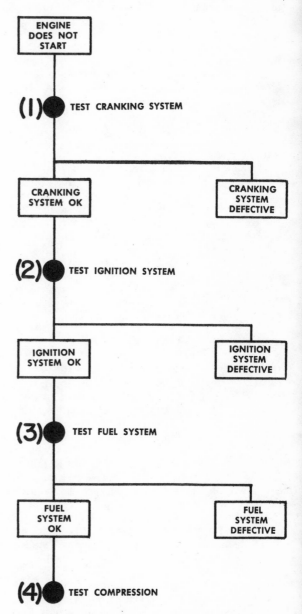

Roadmap for emergency troubleshooting when an engine does not start. The four numbered tests are referred to in the text.

1

area in order to locate the exact source of trouble. The testing program which follows is emergency in nature, requiring no specialized testing equipment; it is recommended only for roadside emergencies. Other sections of this chapter take up the more scientific methods of troubleshooting, using accurate testing equipment.

THE CRANKING SYSTEM (TEST 1)

Turn on the ignition switch and energize the starting motor. If the starting motor cranks the engine at a normal rate of speed, it is an indication that the battery, cables, starting switch, and starting motor are in good shape. A defective cranking system is evidenced by failure of the cranking motor to spin the engine at a normal rate of speed.

If the cranking system is operating satisfactorily, go on to the second test, the ignition system. If it is not operating properly, proceed to the more Detailed Tests of the cranking system which follow this section in order to isolate the trouble.

THE IGNITION SYSTEM (TEST 2)

Disconnect one spark plug wire and hold it about ¼" from the plug terminal while cranking the engine with the ignition switch turned on. A good, constantly occurring spark to the plug means that the ignition system is in good shape. No spark, a weak spark, or an irregularly occurring one means ignition trouble.

If the ignition system is operating satisfactorily, go on to the third test, the fuel system. If it is not operating properly, proceed to the more Detailed Tests of the ignition system which follow this section in order to isolate the trouble.

THE FUEL SYSTEM (TEST 3)

Remove the air cleaner to uncover the carburetor throat. Then open and close the throttle several times. A stream of fuel will be discharged from the accelerating jet if the fuel system is in good shape. No discharge indicates that there is no fuel in the carburetor, which means trouble in the fuel system. In rare instances, the carburetor accelerating system may be defective and no fuel will be discharged even though the carburetor is full of gasoline. Usually there is a decided resistance to movement of the throttle when such a condition exists.

If the fuel system is operating satisfactorily, go on to the fourth test, compression. If it is not operating properly, proceed to the more Detailed Tests of the fuel system to isolate the trouble.

COMPRESSION (TEST 4)

Compression can be checked by removing a spark plug and holding a thumb over the spark plug hole while the engine is being cranked. Good compression produces a distinct pressure under your thumb as the piston rises to the top of its stroke.

Failure of an engine to start due to compression

Testing the ignition system for a spark to the spark plug terminal.

trouble is rarely encountered in the field. Most frequently, compression trouble will show up as defects in but one or two cylinders. No compression in all cylinders of an engine may occur from improper mating of the timing gears when the engine is rebuilt. It can happen on the road through jumping of a loose timing chain or the snapping of a camshaft—but this is so infrequently the case that it can almost be ruled out as a condition causing starting trouble.

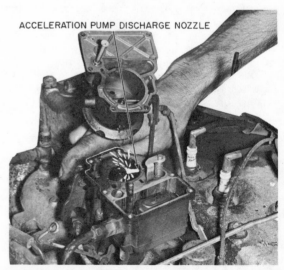

ACCELERATION PUMP DISCHARGE NOZZLE

Testing the fuel system. If there is fuel in the carburetor, it can be seen as a discharge from the pump jet. Generally, it is not necessary to remove the top of the carburetor, because the fuel stream can be seen through the choke bore. The cover was removed in this case for photographic purposes.

DETAILED TESTS FOR HARD STARTING

ISOLATING THE STARTING TROUBLE

The more detailed tests which follow are to isolate the starting trouble in the defective system located by the first series of tests. Each of the four general areas of trouble is broken down further to tests of individual components. In this manner, the exact part causing the trouble can be located and replaced. After the car has been started, it should be driven to the garage, where accurate testing equipment can be used to find the cause of the original breakdown.

CRANKING SYSTEM

The cranking system consists of a battery, cables, starting switch, and the starting motor. Failure of the starting motor to spin the engine, or turning it too slow, is an indication of a defect in one of the above parts.

Battery (Test 1). The battery supplies electric current for the starting motor, lights, ignition, and other electrical accessories. If the starting motor

Testing a cable connection by inserting a screwdriver blade between the battery terminal and the cable connector (Test 2). If the terminal is corroded, the screwdriver blade will make contact between the two parts of the connection.

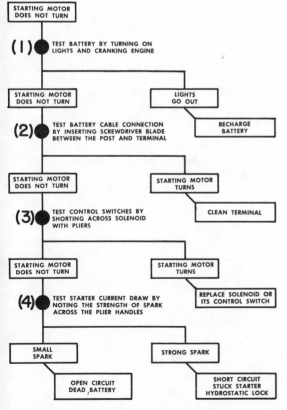

Roadmap for emergency troubleshooting of the cranking system when the starting motor does not turn. The four numbered tests are referred to in the text.

spins the engine at a fairly good rate of speed and then rapidly slows down, the battery is discharged. Turn on the lights while cranking the engine. If the lights go out, the battery is discharged. There is not enough current in a partially charged battery to supply both the starting motor and the lighting system.

A six-volt battery with a defective cell (shorted separator) usually will not turn the starting motor at all, although it may do so for a very short period if the battery has been charged by a recent run of the engine. If such a battery is allowed to stand for a short time, it will lose this surface charge. A twelve-volt battery may operate the starting motor with a defective cell, but it will not spin the starting motor fast enough, and starting troubles will result.

Battery Cables (Test 2). Quite frequently, a bad connection between the battery post and the battery cable will show up as a dead battery. To check this condition, insert a screwdriver blade between the battery post and the cable while having an assistant operate the starting motor switch. Try the blade on each terminal connection. Now, if the starting motor turns, evidently the connection is bad. It should be cleaned by removing the cable terminal and scraping it and the battery post until

STARTING MOTOR SOLENOID

Bridging the solenoid switch (Test 3) should cause the starting motor to operate unless the trouble is in the starting motor itself.

clean metal appears. Then replace and tighten the terminal securely.

Switches (Test 3). A defective switch in the starting circuit can be checked by bridging each switch in turn with a jumper wire or a pair of plier handles. Bridging the solenoid switch bypasses all other control switches, and should energize the starting motor regardless of any other defect in the starting motor control circuit. Use a heavy piece of wire for this test as a thin one will become very hot from the large amount of current drawn through this circuit. Holding a hot wire may cause a serious hand injury.

If the starting motor does not operate with the solenoid switch shorted, and a fully charged battery, then the trouble must be in the starting motor itself.

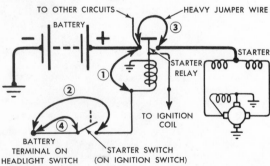

Use a jumper wire to bridge each switch in turn to find an open circuit in the starting motor control system.

Starting Motor (Test 4). The size of the spark across the plier handles in the previous test is an indication of the kind of trouble to be expected. If there is a heavy spark across the handles of the pliers, and the starting motor does not turn, it is possible that the starting motor is stuck to the flywheel, the starting motor has a short circuit, or there is a hydrostatic lock in the engine.

If there is little or no spark across the plier handles as they are moved across the solenoid switch terminals, there is an open circuit present with little or no electricity flowing. This condition can be caused by a dead battery, a poor battery terminal connection, or poor connections at the starting motor brushes due to a burned commutator or one with oil on it. If the starting motor spins, but does not crank the engine, the starting motor drive is defective.

IGNITION SYSTEM

The ignition system furnishes the electric spark which fires the mixture. Absence of a spark, or a weak spark, will cause starting trouble. Ignition troubles should be isolated by logical testing. For this purpose, the system is broken into its smaller circuits; the primary and secondary. Each of these should be broken down further and individual components tested separately.

To Test the Entire Ignition System. Remove one spark plug wire and hold it about $\frac{1}{2}$" away from the base of the spark plug or any metallic part of the engine. Crank the engine with the ignition switch turned on. A good spark from the wire to the metal means that the entire ignition system is in good working order. No spark, or a weak, irregularly occurring spark, means ignition trouble which must be traced by means of the following tests:

To Test the Primary Circuit (Test 1). Loosen the distributor cap retaining bails and move the cap to one side. Remove the rotor. Turn the engine over by means of the fan belt or starting motor until the contact points close. Turn on the ignition switch. Remove the high tension wire leading to the center of the distributor cap; this is the main wire from the ignition coil which supplies the high voltage to the rotor for distribution to the spark plugs. Hold this wire about $\frac{1}{2}$" from any metallic part of the engine. Open and close the contact points with a screwdriver. Hold the screwdriver against the movable point only as shown. A good, regularly occurring spark from the high tension wire to ground means a good primary circuit and a good ignition coil. No spark, or a weak erratic one, from the high tension wire to ground means primary circuit trouble or a bad ignition coil.

To Test the Ignition Contact Points (Test 2). To test the condition of the ignition contact set, turn the engine over with the fan belt or starting

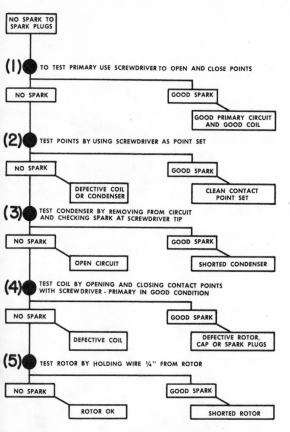

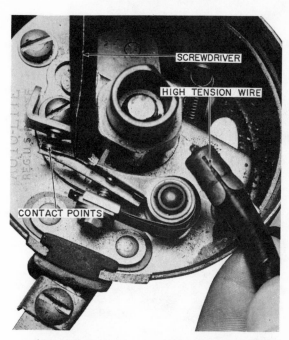

Opening and closing the ignition points with a screwdriver (Test 1), while holding the main high tension wire close to a metallic part of the engine, is a simple test of the primary circuit efficiency.

Roadmap for emergency troubleshooting of the ignition system. The five numbered tests are referred to in the text.

motor until the contact points are separated. Slide the screwdriver blade up and down, making contact between the movable point and the bottom plate of the distributor, as shown. You are now using the screwdriver tip and the bottom plate of the distributor as a set of contact points. A good spark from the high tension wire to the ground, after having had no spark in Test 1, means that you have a defective set of contact points. No spark, or a weak one, means primary circuit trouble, other than the ignition contact points, or a bad ignition coil.

To Test the Condenser (Test 3). A shorted condenser can be checked by noting in the previous ignition contact point test (Test 2), whether or not the tip of the screwdriver blade sparked against the ground plate as it was slid up and down. No spark at the tip of the blade means either a shorted condenser or a break in the primary circuit.

This can be checked further by disconnecting the condenser case where it is screwed to the distributor (do not disconnect the condenser wire lead). Hold the condenser so that its case does not make contact with any metallic part of the distributor.

Using the screwdriver as a set of points (Test 2). Use a cleaned insulator (arrow) to keep the points apart, and then slide the screwdriver blade up and down to make intermittent contact with the point plate.

A sample of good ignition contact points (top), and a bad set (bottom) for comparison. A light gray contact surface is indicative of a set of contact points working at high efficiency. The lower set is burned black from either high voltage or oil.

spark here (with no spark to the spark plugs) means that the trouble must be in the distributor cap, rotor, or spark plugs. It is seldom that spark plug high tension wires (unless obviously rotted) will keep an engine from starting. To check the main high tension wire, from the coil to the center of the distributor cap, replace it with a new piece of high tension wire, or remove the old wire from the metal conduit and repeat Test 4 while keeping the suspected wire away from any grounded surface.

To Test the Distributor Rotor (Test 5). Test the distributor rotor by replacing it on the distributor shaft and holding the main high tension wire (from the coil) about ¼″ from the top of the rotor. With the ignition switch turned on, crank the engine with the starter. If the high tension spark jumps to the rotor, it is grounded (defective); if not, the cap must be defective. Inspect the cap for carbon tracks which indicate the passing of high voltage electricity.

Repeat the test of moving the screwdriver blade up and down while holding it against the movable point. Be sure that the contact points are open while making this test. A spark at the screwdriver tip now, which was not present with the condenser in the circuit, means that the condenser is shorted out.

No spark at the screwdriver tip with the condenser out of the circuit means that there is an open circuit somewhere in the primary. Check the small wire lead from the primary terminal to the movable contact point. This wire lead sometimes parts under the constant flexing of operation.

To Test the Secondary Circuit (Test 4). The secondary circuit cannot be tested until the primary circuit is functioning perfectly. If the primary circuit tests good, or after the necessary repairs have been made to the primary circuit, then the secondary circuit can be tested.

To test the secondary circuit, turn the engine over until the contact points close. Then turn on the ignition switch. Hold the main high tension wire (from the center terminal of the distributor cap) about ½″ from any metallic part of the engine. Open and close the contact points with a screwdriver blade held against the movable contact point only. No spark, or a weak one, from the wire to the block (*with a good primary circuit*), means a bad ignition coil or a defective main high tension wire from the coil to the distributor (especially where it runs through metal conduit). A good

A broken primary lead may not show up until you pull on it. The insulation hides the damage.

A cracked distributor cap always shows these characteristic carbon tracks. A crack between two terminals will cause misfiring, but a crack from the center terminal to the outside will prevent the engine from starting. Cracks often start from moisture on the surface of the insulating material.

FUEL SYSTEM

The purpose of the fuel system is to bring a combustible mixture of gasoline and air into the cylinders. The fuel system consists of the fuel tank, the fuel pump, and the carburetor. Troubles in the fuel system can be caused by too little fuel in the combustion chambers—or too much.

Too Little Fuel: TESTING THE FUEL PUMP OUTPUT (TEST 1). Disconnect the fuel line leading into the carburetor bowl and hold a container under the line to catch the gasoline as it spurts from the open end. (The ignition switch should be off; otherwise, the high tension wire should be removed from the center of the distributor cap to prevent the possibility of the engine starting and spraying gasoline all over the engine compartment.) If a good size stream of fuel flows from the pipe, and the trouble has been isolated to the fuel system, the defect must be in the carburetor. If no fuel flows, the trouble must be in the pump, lines, or gas tank.

It is seldom that the carburetor itself causes starting trouble. Instances have been found of an inlet strainer plugged, or the float valve needle stuck in the closed position, but these are exceptions. Cases of an automatic choke not functioning are encountered more frequently in starting trouble. If the automatic choke does not close on a cold engine being cranked, hold your hand over the top of the carburetor bore to restrict the flow of air, which will assist in starting the engine.

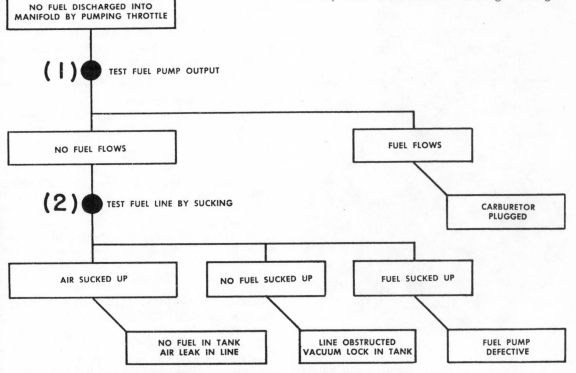

Roadmap for emergency troubleshooting of the fuel system. The two numbered tests are referred to in the text.

Testing the fuel pump output (Test 1). Cranking the engine with the starting motor should produce a full-sized stream of fuel each time the pump pulses.

The spark plugs of an overchoked engine will be wet with fuel.

Where the choke sticks in the closed position, it can be opened with your fingers and held open until the engine is firing properly.

To TEST THE GAS TANK AND LINES (TEST 2). To check the tank and lines, the fuel line should be disconnected at the inlet side of the fuel pump and sucked on to check for obstructions. Sucking on this line should bring up a mouthful of liquid fuel if there are no defects in the line or tank. Be sure to empty your mouth immediately and wash it out with water, if possible. If liquid fuel can be sucked up, and there is no flow out of the fuel pump, then the fuel pump is defective and must be repaired or replaced.

If only air is obtained by sucking on the line, then there is no fuel in the tank or there is an air leak in the line, probably at the flexible line leading into the fuel pump. If sucking on the line feels solid, and no fuel can be drawn up, the trouble is due to an obstruction in the line or a plugged gas tank vent.

Too Much Fuel. Too much fuel can be caused by overchoking, a defective float, or a defective needle and seat in the carburetor allowing fuel to by-pass the needle and overflow into the intake manifold. This can be seen as a steady stream of raw gasoline coming out of the main jet when the engine is being cranked. Raw gasoline may also enter the intake manifold in excessive amounts when the engine is stopped after a very hard and prolonged pull. In this case, the heat developed by the engine may cause the fuel to boil within the float chamber of the carburetor and percolate over the top of the main delivery tube into the intake manifold. Some carburetors are vented to prevent this possibility, but there are times when this vent is not functioning properly. Excessive amounts of raw gasoline can be seen by opening the throttle fully and looking down into the intake manifold through the carburetor bore.

Sometimes black smoke coming from the exhaust pipe while the engine is being started is another sign of too much fuel. The best test, however, is the removal of a spark plug. An overchoked engine will have spark plugs wet with raw gasoline while a normal engine will have dry spark plugs.

To start an engine which has been overloaded with fuel, it is necessary first to remedy the condition causing the trouble, and then the engine can be started by opening the throttle fully, which opens the choke. Under no circumstances should the throttle be pumped, as this will force additional quantities of raw fuel into the intake manifold.

TROUBLESHOOTING THE MECHANICAL PARTS OF THE ENGINE

Troubleshooting is performed before the engine is disassembled so that the mechanic can give the car owner an estimate of the cost of the repair job before work is started. This troubleshooting mate-

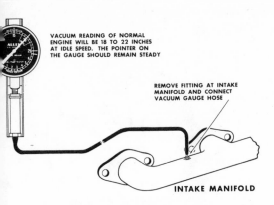

VACUUM READING OF NORMAL ENGINE WILL BE 18 TO 22 INCHES AT IDLE SPEED. THE POINTER ON THE GAUGE SHOULD REMAIN STEADY

REMOVE FITTING AT INTAKE MANIFOLD AND CONNECT VACUUM GAUGE HOSE

INTAKE MANIFOLD

vacuum gauge is a very important testing device. It is connected to the intake manifold.

al will also be useful in assisting a mechanic to lve those few minor defects which sometimes ocr after a reconditioning job, even after meticuus care has been taken in rebuilding the engine. most cases, it is just some little thing causing e engine to lose power, overheat, knock, pump l, or lose compression.

Two very important gauges are needed to locate echanical engine defects: a vacuum and a comression gauge. The vacuum gauge measures the mount of vacuum in the intake manifold and is excellent indicator of the over-all efficiency of e engine. A great many engine mechanical dects can be identified with a vacuum gauge. The mpression gauge is used to identify the exact linder in which a compression defect exists.

SING A VACUUM GAUGE

The vacuum gauge is connected to the intake anifold through the windshield wiper hose fitting. he engine should be run until it is at operating mperature and then idled to obtain a reading.

CORRECTIONS. A vacuum gauge indicates the fference between the pressure inside the intake anifold and the atmospheric pressure outside. It calibrated in inches of mercury (Hg). Conseuently, the reading will be affected by any varition in atmospheric pressure, such as altitude and eather conditions; therefore, the most important ing about a vacuum gauge is the action of the eedle rather than a theoretical numerical reading. enerally speaking, the vacuum gauge reading will e 1″ lower for each 1000′ of elevation.

NORMAL ENGINE. A normal engine will show a auge reading of 18″–22″ Hg with the pointer teady. Eight-cylinder engines will read toward he high side whereas six- and four-cylinder engines ill read closer to the low side. On many later odel cars, with overlapping valve timing, the auge needle will fluctuate widely. To overcome his, many gauges have a constrictor valve which

can be adjusted until the fluctuations are reduced to the width of the pointer tip. On gauges without this valve, the hose can be pinched until the undesirable fluctuations cease.

LEAKING VALVE. If a valve is leaking, the pointer will drop from 1″–7″ at regular intervals whenever the defective valve attempts to close during idle.

STICKING VALVE. A sticking valve is indicated by a rapid, intermittent drop each time the valve is supposed to close when the engine is idling. A sticky valve condition can be pinpointed by applying a small amount of penetrating oil or lacquer thinner to each guide in turn. When the sticky valve is reached, the situation will be remedied temporarily.

WEAK OR BROKEN VALVE SPRING. If the pointer fluctuates rapidly between 10″ and 22″ Hg at 2000 rpm, and the fluctuations increase as engine speed is increased, weak valve springs are indicated. If a valve spring is broken, the pointer will fluctuate rapidly every time the valve attempts to close at idle.

WORN VALVE GUIDES. Worn valve guides admit air which upsets carburetion. The vacuum gauge reading will be lower than normal with fluctuations of about 3″ Hg on each side of normal when the engine is idling.

PISTON RING DEFECTS. Open the throttle and allow the engine to pick up speed to about 2000 rpm, and then close the throttle quickly. The pointer should jump from about 2″ to 5″ or more of Hg above the normal reading if the rings are in good condition. A lower gain should be investigated by making a compression test to localize trouble.

BLOWN CYLINDER HEAD GASKET. The pointer will drop sharply 10″ Hg from a normal reading and return each time the defective cylinders reach firing position with the engine idling.

INCORRECT IDLE AIR-FUEL MIXTURE. When the needle drifts slowly back and forth on idle, the fuel mixture is too rich. A lean mixture will cause an irregular drop of the needle.

INTAKE MANIFOLD AIR LEAKS. If there are any air leaks in the induction system, the needle will drop from 3″ to 9″ Hg below normal with the engine idling, but will remain quite steady.

RESTRICTED EXHAUST SYSTEM. Open the throttle until about 2000 rpm is reached. Close the throttle quickly. If there is no excessive back pressure, the pointer will drop to not less than 2″ Hg, increase to 25″ Hg and then return to normal quickly. If the gauge does not register 5″ Hg or more above the normal reading, and the needle seems to stop momentarily in its return, the exhaust system is partially restricted.

LATE IGNITION TIMING. A low steady reading on idle indicates late ignition timing or a uniformly close setting of the tappet adjustments. The timing must never be set with a vacuum gauge; use a timing light for accuracy.

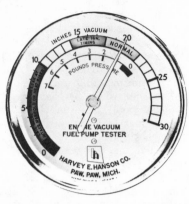

A normal engine will show a gauge reading of 18"–22" Hg, with the needle remaining quite steady.

Weak valve springs will cause wide fluctuations of the needle.

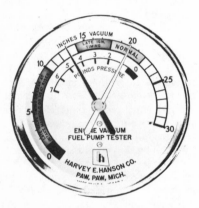

A burned valve will cause the needle to drop sharply each time the valve tries to close.

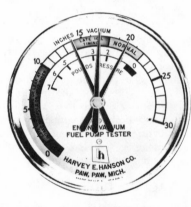

Worn valve guides admit air which upsets carburetion. The needle will fluctuate slowly.

A sticky valve will cause the needle to drop sharply each time the valve tries to close, but not as much as the burned valve.

Piston ring defects can be determined by a low reading on the gauge when the throttle is closed rapidly after speeding up the engine.

A blown cylinder head gasket will cause sharp drops of the needle.

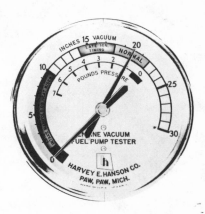

A restricted exhaust will cause a momentary stop to the return of the needle when the throttle is closed quickly.

A rich air-fuel mixture on idle will cause the needle to drift back and forth.

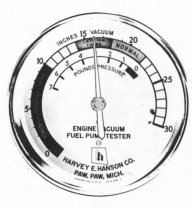

Late ignition timing is evidenced by a low but steady reading.

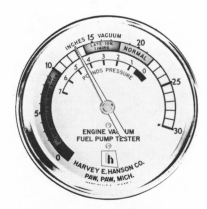

An intake manifold gasket air leak will lower the reading from 3" to 9" Hg.

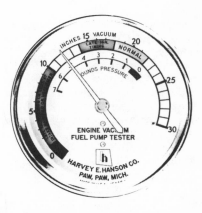

Late valve timing is evidenced by a low, steady reading, but lower than late ignition timing.

A compression gauge is important for checking the valve and ring condition. In practice, an equal number of pulses are recorded.

LATE VALVE TIMING. A steady but very low reading is generally caused by late ignition timing or late valve timing. If advancing the ignition timing does not increase the gauge reading to normal, then the valve timing is out of adjustment.

USING A COMPRESSION GAUGE

Another very important engine testing gauge is the compression tester. It measures the pressure within the cylinder in pounds per square inch (psi). As with the vacuum gauge, the theoretical numerical reading is not so important as the variation between cylinders. The cylinder pressures should not vary over 15 psi; otherwise, the engine cannot be tuned properly. Variations cause uneven idling and loss of power.

To use the gauge, remove all the spark plugs and insert the rubber tip into each spark plug hole in turn. With the throttle held wide open, crank the engine to obtain about 6 power impulses on the gauge; record the reading. Do this at each cylinder and compare the results. Generally, modern high-compression engines have a reading close to 175 psi. If one cylinder is low, insert a tablespoonful of heavy oil on top of the piston. Turn the engine over several times to work the oil around the piston rings, and then repeat the test. If the pressure shows a decided increase, there is a compression loss past the piston and rings. If the pressure does not increase, the valves are seating improperly. A defective cylinder head gasket will show a loss of compression in two adjacent cylinders.

LOW-COMPRESSION TROUBLESHOOTING CHART

TROUBLES & CAUSES

1. Valves
   1a. Insufficient tappet clearance
   1b. Sticking valves
   1c. Warped heads or bent stems
   1d. Burned, pitted, or distorted valve faces and seats
   1e. Weak or broken valve springs
   1f. Distortion of cylinder head and/or block caused by uneven tightening of the bolts
   1g. Incorrect valve timing
2. Pistons and rings
   2a. Excessive clearance between pistons and cylinder walls
   2b. Eccentric or tapered cylinder bores
   2c. Scored cylinder walls
   2d. Scored pistons
   2e. Broken pistons
   2f. Scuffed rings
   2g. Insufficient piston ring end gaps
   2h. Stuck piston rings
   2i. Binding of rings due to "set" caused by mechanic overstretching during installation
   2j. Insufficient piston ring-to-wall tension due to weak expanders
   2k. Ring lands worn unevenly
   2l. Ring grooves too deep for the expanders used
   2m. Standard rings installed in oversize bores
   2n. Top rings running dry because oil control rings are too severe
   2o. Top rings running dry because of gasoline dilution caused by stuck manifold heat control
   2p. Abrasive dust left in cylinder bores from honing or grinding valves
3. Gaskets
   3a. Warped head and/or block
   3b. Blown-out cylinder head gasket
   3c. Cylinder head bolts tightened unevenly
   3d. Incorrect type of gasket

TROUBLESHOOTING FOR EXCESSIVE OIL CONSUMPTION

Oil can be consumed in the combustion chamber or lost through leaks. If the engine is actually burning oil, a blue-gray smoke will emerge from the exhaust pipe whenever the engine is accelerated, especially after it has idled for a short period of time. Fouled spark plugs are a good indication that oil is being burned in the combustion chambers.

Oil can pass into the combustion areas in only four ways: it can go past the piston rings, the valve guides, the vacuum booster pump, or it can pass through a defective crankcase ventilation system. Leaks can be caused by defective or improperly installed gaskets, by excessive crankcase pressures caused by blow-by, or by plugging of the crankcase ventilating system. Unless the vents are clean, blow-by pressures can force enough oil vapors from the crankcase to cause a noticeable increase in oil consumption.

OIL LEAKS

Fresh oil on any engine housing usually washes the dirt from that part and is an excellent indication that oil is leaking from that area. Washed areas on the ventilator side of the chassis usually

Oil leaks can be pinpointed by mixing a special fluorescent powder with the oil, and then shining a blacklight under the pan to locate the source of the leak.

are caused by oil being blown or sucked out of the crankcase. It is surprising just how much oil can be lost through a small leak. One drop of oil every hundred feet causes an oil loss of a quart per thousand miles. Note how the center of each driving lane is covered with oil from external leaks, and you will realize the need for checking this loss. Note that these drippings are much heavier on an upgrade due to blow-by pressures forcing the oil through defective gaskets and bearings.

VACUUM BOOSTER PUMP

Some engines are equipped with a vacuum booster pump which assists in the operation of the windshield wiper. This pump can be a source of considerable oil consumption. When the diaphragm

of such a pump ruptures, or becomes porous, the intake manifold vacuum of between 18″ and 25″ Hg sucks oil vapors into the combustion areas. Originally, these pumps were mounted with the vacuum side down, in which case a defective diaphragm sucked huge quantities of oil into the intake manifold. The pump has now been mounted in an inverted position, in which case a leaky diaphragm will draw in oil vapors and air. The oil vapors increase oil consumption while the air leaks upset carburetion.

There are several ways to check a suspected booster pump. A good quick test is to turn on the windshield wiper with the engine idling (first wet the windshield to avoid scratching the glass). Accelerate the engine; if the wiper blades stop, it is a sure sign of a ruptured diaphragm. Another quick test is to disconnect the pipe where it enters the intake manifold. The presence of lubricating oil in the tube also indicates a defective diaphragm.

A very accurate testing method, which can be used without removing the pump, requires a vacuum pump and gauge such as is furnished with distributor analyzers. Disconnect both vacuum pump pipes and remove the fittings. Install a 1/8″ pipe plug in the windshield wiper side and a hose fitting in the manifold side of the pump. Tighten the diaphragm screws securely. Connect the vacuum pump and gauge to the manifold side of the pump. Operate the test vacuum pump until the gauge reaches 18″ Hg of vacuum. If the diaphragms are in good shape, the gauge will maintain its reading. If the diaphragms are porous, the gauge will not read over 12″ Hg. If the diaphragms are ruptured, the gauge will not read over 2″ Hg.

The blacklight is moved about until the source of the leak is located by a glow as the lamp causes the oil to fluoresce.

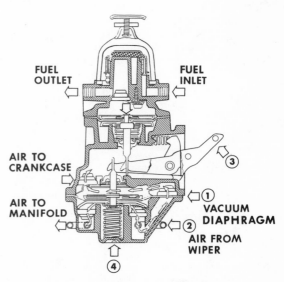

A vacuum booster pump is often used to operate the windshield wipers. A ruptured diaphragm can be the source of considerable oil consumption as the pump is connected to the intake manifold.

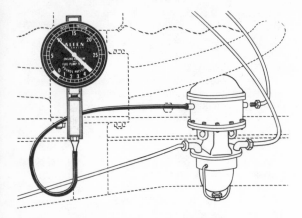

A vacuum gauge can be connected to the pump output to test the diaphragm. A good pump will hold better than 10" Hg.

CRANKCASE VENTILATOR

On road-draft type crankcase ventilating systems, clogged inlet breather caps and plugged vents in the outlet tube increase the crankcase pressures and so contribute to oil leaks.

Where a positive-type crankcase ventilating system is used, clogging of the metering valve, located in the line between the crankcase and the intake manifold, will cause crankcase pressure to increase which will force the oil out from around the pan gaskets and oil seals. If the valve sticks open, large quantities of oil vapors will be drawn into the combustion areas under high-vacuum operating conditions with resulting high oil consumption.

Since oil can be lost in any combination of the above ways, it is necessary for the mechanic to examine the engine carefully before it is disassembled. After disassembly has started, it is much more difficult to check many of these things.

EXCESSIVE OIL CONSUMPTION TROUBLE-SHOOTING CHART

TROUBLES & CAUSES

1. **Piston and ring defects**
   1a. Piston improperly fitted or finished
   1b. Snaky piston ring grooves
   1c. Ring grooves worn overwidth or flared
   1d. Insufficient number of drain holes in oil ring grooves
   1e. Drain holes in oil ring grooves too small
   1f. Broken ring
   1g. Piston with wrong cam-grind
   1h. Badly worn or collapsed pistons
   1i. Scuffed rings
   1j. Improper seating of rings in grooves
   1k. Insufficient clearance at ring gap
   1l. Insufficient ring tension
   1m. Out-of-round rings from improper installation

1n. Warped or twisted rings from improper installation
1o. Not enough side clearance between rings and grooves
1p. Compression rings installed upside down
1q. Wrong size rings
1r. Insufficient ventilation in oil rings
1s. Slots in oil rings clogged
1t. Piston and connecting rod assembly out of alignment
1u. Excessive clearance between piston and cylinder bore

2. **Bearing defects**
   2a. Scored rod bearings
   2b. Spurt holes in rods with worn bearings adding to excessive bearing throw-off
   2c. Worn crankshaft throws
   2d. Worn main bearing oil seals
   2e. Excessive clearance

3. **Valve guide defects**
   3a. Worn valve guides
   3b. Intake valve guides installed upside down
   3c. Valve stem oil seals incorrectly installed or worn

4. **Cylinder bore defects**
   4a. Excessively worn, tapered, or out-of-round cylinder bores
   4b. Wavy cylinder bores caused by heat distortion or uneven tightening of head bolts
   4c. Ring ledge at top or bottom of cylinder bore
   4d. Scored cylinder bores
   4e. Rough finish on cylinder walls causing rapid ring wear
   4f. Cylinder block out of alignment with crankshaft

5. **Crankcase defects**
   5a. Main bearing oil return pipe clogged
   5b. Oil level too high
   5c. Broken pipe in oil line spraying oil into cylinder bores
   5d. Clogged breather pipe
   5e. Stuck valve in positive-type crankcase ventilating system
   5f. Excessive crankcase pressures caused by blow-by
   5g. Improper reading of dip stick (not pushed in fully)

6. **Vacuum pump defects**
   6a. Diaphragm punctured
   6b. Loose fuel pump
   6c. Broken fuel pump gaskets
   6d. Defective fuel pump oil seal

7. **Lubrication defects**
   7a. Poor grade of oil
   7b. Thin or diluted oil
   7c. Dirty oil containing abrasives causing excessive wear
   7d. High oil pressure
   7e. Rocker arm oil drain sealed off

8. **Defects causing overheating resulting in excessive oil consumption**
   8a. Carburetor mixture too lean
   8b. Improperly timed valves
   8c. Cooling system defects
   8d. Late ignition timing

TROUBLESHOOTING FOR ENGINE NOISES

One of the more difficult problems facing the mechanic is the locating of foreign noises. Engine noises vary in intensity and frequency, depending on their source. It is difficult to describe engine noises with mere words. Experience will have to be built up, using the descriptions which follow as a guide.

The only tools which the mechanic has to help him locate the source of an engine noise are a screwdriver to short out spark plugs and a stethoscope or listening rod to carry the sound directly to his ear.

CRANKSHAFT KNOCKS

Noises classified as crankshaft knocks are usually dull, heavy metallic knocks which increase in frequency as the speed and load on the engine are increased. Or they may become more noticeable at extremely low speed when the engine is idling unevenly.

The most common crankshaft knock, due to excessive clearance, is usually apparent as an audible "bump" under the following conditions: when the engine is pulling hard, when an engine is started, during acceleration, or at speeds above 35 mph. If excessive clearance exists at only one or two of the crankshaft journals, the "bump" will be less frequent and less pronounced. Usually, alternate short circuiting of each spark plug will determine the approximate location of a loose bearing.

Excessive crankshaft end-play causes a sharp rap to occur at irregular intervals, usually at idling speeds, and, in bad cases, can be detected by the alternate release and engagement of the clutch. To detect a loose flywheel, advance the engine idle to a road speed equivalent to 15 mph. Turn off the ignition switch and, when the engine has almost stopped, turn the switch on again. If this operation is repeated several times and if, of course, the flywheel is loose, one distinct knock will be noted every time the switch is turned on.

CONNECTING ROD BEARING NOISES

Connecting rod bearing noises are usually a light rap or clatter of much less intensity than main bearing knocks. The noise is most audible when the engine is "floating" or running with a light load at approximately 25 mph. The noise becomes louder as engine speed is increased. Connecting rod bearing knocks can be located best by grounding out each of the spark plugs, one at a time. Generally, the noise cannot be eliminated entirely by a short circuit, but ordinarily will be reduced considerably in intensity.

PISTON NOISES

The commonest piston noise is a slap due to the rocking of the piston from side to side in the cylinder. Although, in some engines, piston slap causes a clicking noise, usually it is a hollow, muffled, bell-like sound. Slight piston noises that occur when the engine is cold, and disappear after the engine is warm, do not ordinarily warrant correction. Piston ring noises generally cause a click, a snap, or a sharp rattle on acceleration.

Short circuit each spark plug to locate piston and ring noises. As this test will affect other engine noises, sometimes the result is confusing. To detect piston slap more accurately, drive the car at low speeds under a load. The noise generally increases in intensity as the throttle is opened and additional load applied. On some engines, with very loose pistons, a piston rattle is encountered at speeds between 30–50 mph when the engine is not being accelerated.

To eliminate piston and ring noises momentarily, put 1–2 oz. of very heavy engine oil into each cylinder through the spark plug hole. Crank the engine for several revolutions with the ignition switch turned off until the oil works itself down past the piston rings. Then install the spark plugs, start the engine, and determine whether or not the noise still exists.

PISTON PIN NOISES

The commonest piston pin noise is the result of excessive piston pin clearance. This causes a sharp, metallic, double-knock, generally audible with the engine idling. On some engines, however, the noise is more noticeable at car speeds of 25–35 mph. Interference between the upper end of the connecting rod and the pin boss (bossing) is difficult to diagnose and can be mistaken for a valve lifter noise.

To test for piston pin noises, allow the engine to run at idle speed. In most cases, a sharp metallic double-knock will become more evident when the

A stethoscope or a listening rod is handy to locate the source of engine noises.

spark plug, in the cylinder with the loose piston pin, is shorted out. Retarding the spark will generally re-reduce the intensity of the knock. If the pins in all pistons are loose, a metallic rattle, which is impossible to short out in any one cylinder, will be heard.

VALVE MECHANISM NOISES

Noisy valve mechanism has a characteristic clicking sound occurring at regular intervals. Inasmuch as the valves are operating at half crankshaft speed, the frequency of valve action noise is generally lower than that of other engine noises.

To determine whether the noise is due to excessive valve clearance, insert a feeler gauge between the valve stem and the rocker arm or tappet. If the noise stops, the clearance is probably excessive and the adjusting screw should be adjusted. Never reduce the clearance to below factory specification or the valve will burn.

A sticky valve will cause a clicking sound similar to a loose tappet adjustment which comes and goes according to driving conditions. A sticky valve can be detected by driving the car hard until the engine is well heated. Then quickly allow the engine to idle. If there is a sticky valve, the clicking will become quite pronounced but will lessen gradually and sometimes disappear as the engine returns to normal operating temperature. The noise is accompanied by a rhythmic jerk due to the misfiring cylinder. As the noise disappears, so does the jerk, and the engine will finally smooth out as the valve seats.

To locate a noisy hydraulic valve lifter, place a finger on each valve spring cap in succession. A distinct shock will be felt when the valve returns to its seat if the lifter is not functioning properly.

A loose timing gear generally can be detected by a sharp clatter at low engine speeds with an uneven idle. When testing for this condition, short circuit one or two spark plugs to produce the necessary rough idle.

SPARK KNOCK

Preignition, or spark knock, causes a metallic ringing sound, often described as a "ping." Usually, it is encountered when the engine is laboring, being accelerated rapidly, or is overheated. Preignition is caused by an incandescent particle of carbon or metal in the combustion chamber igniting the mixture prematurely while the piston is coming up on the compression stroke. This results in very heavy pressure being applied to the piston at the wrong time, causing the piston, the connecting rod, and the bearing to vibrate, and resulting in the sound known as "spark knock."

Detonation is caused most frequently by a fuel of too low an octane rating. It burns too rapidly, resulting in sudden and abnormal pressure against the piston.

To locate a noisy hydraulic valve lifter, place your finger on each rocker arm in turn with the engine idling. You can feel the shock if the lifter is defective.

ACCESSORY NOISES

Noises in the alternator or water pump can be checked by removing the drive belt for a short operating period. If the noise remains, it is not in the alternator or the water pump.

ENGINE NOISE TROUBLESHOOTING CHART

TROUBLES & CAUSES

1. **Crankshaft knocks**
   1a. Excessive bearing clearance
   1b. Excessive end-play
   1c. Eccentric or out-of-round journals
   1d. Sprung crankshaft
   1e. Bearing misalignment
   1f. Insufficient oil supply
   1g. Restricted oil supply to one main bearing
   1h. Low oil pressure
   1i. Badly diluted oil
   1j. Loose flywheel
   1k. Loose impulse neutralizer
   1l. Broken crankshaft web
2. **Connecting rod bearing knocks**
   2a. Excessive bearing clearance
   2b. Out-of-round crankpin journals
   2c. Misaligned connecting rods
   2d. Top of connecting rod bolt turned around and striking the camshaft
   2e. Insufficient oil supply
   2f. Low oil pressure
   2g. Badly diluted oil
3. **Piston noises**
   3a. Collapsed piston skirt
   3b. Excessive piston-to-cylinder bore clearance
   3c. Eccentric or tapered cylinder bores
   3d. Piston pin too tight
   3e. Connecting rod misalignment
   3f. Piston or rings hitting ridge at top of cylinder bore

3g. Piston striking carbon accumulation at top of cylinder bore

3h. Piston striking cylinder head gasket

3i. Broken piston ring

3j. Excessive side clearance between a ring and its groove

3k. Piston pin hole out of square with the piston

3l. Ring lands not properly relieved

4. **Piston pin noises**

4a. Excessive piston pin clearance

4b. Loose piston pin locking screw

4c. Piston pin rubbing against cylinder wall

4d. Top end of connecting rod bossing

4e. Tight pin causing piston to slap

5. **Valve mechanism noises**

5a. Excessive clearance between valve stem and tappet or rocker arm

5b. Sticky valve

5c. Excessive clearance between tappet and block

5d. Lower end of lifter scored or broken

5e. Tappet screw or rocker arm face pitted

5f. Weak or broken valve spring

5g. Inverted valve spring

5h. Warped valve head

5i. Valve seat not concentric with guide

5j. Excessive stem-to-guide clearance

5k. End of valve stem not faced square

5l. Weak rocker arm spacer spring

5m. Loose timing gear

6. **Spark knock**

6a. Low octane fuel

6b. Excessive carbon deposits

6c. Ignition timed too early

6d. Excessively lean air-fuel mixture

6e. Weak automatic advance weight springs

6f. Manifold heat control valve stuck in closed position

6g. Spark plugs too hot

6h. Burned spark plug porcelain

6i. Sharp metallic edges in combustion chamber

6j. Cylinder head gasket projecting into combustion chamber

6k. Overheated valves

6l. Excessive engine coolant temperatures

6m. Loose fan belt

UNDER-HOOD NOISE TESTS

TROUBLES & TESTS

1. **Belts**

1a. Low-speed squish. Squirt water on belts to eliminate the noise temporarily. Clean the belt and pulley.

1b. High-speed loaded alternator belt squeal. Check belt for glazed or burned sidewalls. Tighten belt or replace as necessary. *NOTE: To load the alternator, turn on the lights, radio, heater, etc. and accelerate engine in neutral.*

2. **Water pump**

2a. Seal squawk that occurs at idle or just above. The noise is erratic and sensitive to minor speed changes, and will usually disappear at faster engine speeds. Use water pump lubricant to correct.

2b. Water pump bearing failure. Noise is present at water pump at all engine speeds. Use listening rod or stethoscope to locate noise.

Generally, bearing looseness can be felt by applying pressure in various directions to the fan blades.

2c. Bearing rattle that develops at a narrow engine speed band just above idle. It can be eliminated by increasing or decreasing engine speed. The only correction is to replace the bearings.

3. **Power steering**

3a. Various sounds that come from the power steering can be checked by removing the drive belt.

4. **Accessory bracket noises**

4a. Various sounds can be from a rattle to a buzzing noise. Check the bracket to make sure that all bolts are tight and not bottomed in the tapped holes.

5. **Engine noises**

5a. Crankcase ventilator valve buzz or hiss. Pinch vent hose to check valve action.

5b. Engine oil pump buzz or rattle. Erratic and usually difficult to reproduce, but is present with alternator belt removed. Overhaul oil pump to eliminate noise.

5c. Manifold heat control valve rattle. Hold screwdriver against the valve shaft to dampen noise. Repair heat control to remedy.

5d. Crankshaft seal squeak, fuel pump noise, or tappet noises will be present with alternator and power steering belt removed.

6. **Alternator noises**

6a. Electrical noise such as a whine or buzz can be temporarily eliminated by removing field wire. Turn slip rings and replace brushes.

6b. Loose rear mounting leg bushing noise. Pry against rear alternator leg with rod or screwdriver to eliminate the rattle. Tighten bolt.

6c. Bearing noise that varies from harsh to a siren sound. It is always present at any speed and can be pinpointed to either the front or rear bearing by probing with a stethoscope. The noise can be made to come and go by loosening the alternator adjusting strap and loading and unloading the unit against the drive belt. Replace the bearing(s).

6d. Very loud annoying squealing sound during cold weather. This annoying sound generally appears at about 0° F. but has been heard as high as 20° F. It goes away when the engine becomes heated and reappears when cool. The noise is speed sensitive and can be eliminated temporarily by loosening the drive belt. Replace both bearings to correct.

TROUBLESHOOTING FOR POOR PERFORMANCE DUE TO EXCESSIVE FRICTION

Excessive friction is a frequent contributing cause of power losses; tight rings are perhaps the greatest offender. In an attempt to stop oil pumping, severe expander springs are frequently used behind piston rings. These rings create such excessive cylinder wall friction that power and gas mileage drop amazingly. The best test of a tight engine is to hold the throttle open to an engine speed of approximately 1000 rpm. Keep the accelerator pedal steady and shut off the ignition. Watch the fan blades to see whether or not the engine rocks as it comes to a stop. A tight engine will stop with a "jerk" while a normal engine will rock back and forth on compression.

EXCESSIVE-FRICTION TROUBLE-SHOOTING CHART
TROUBLES & CAUSES
1. **Engine conditions**
   1a. Piston ring expanders too severe
   1b. Piston expanders too severe
   1c. Piston slots not completed
   1d. Wrong cam grind on pistons
   1e. Insufficient piston-to-cylinder wall clearance
   1f. Insufficient piston ring end gap
   1g. Top ring lands not relieved
   1h. Too tight a bearing fit
2. **Miscellaneous conditions**
   2a. Dragging brakes
   2b. Tight wheel bearings
   2c. Misaligned wheels
   2d. Underinflated tires
   2e. Reversed stator installation in turbine of automatic transmission

TROUBLESHOOTING THE COOLING SYSTEM

The cooling system is thermostatically controlled to regulate the engine operating temperature to provide for a short warm-up period. Engine overheating and slow warm-up are the two engine troubles most commonly attributed to the cooling system.

OVERHEATING
Loss of coolant, the accumulation of rust and scale in the coolant chambers, and the passing of hot exhaust gases into the coolant through an internal leak are the main causes of overheating.

On some cars with automatic transmissions, a

By moving the special blacklight around, the exact point of the leak can be located.

leak may develop between the transmission oil cooler and the radiator, allowing oil to bleed into the coolant. Leaks of this nature may be detected visually by removing the radiator cap and inspecting the condition of the coolant.

Loss of coolant can be checked visually by the red rust stains that often form around the leak area. Loss of coolant through an internal crack is often detected by noting the condition of the oil on the dip stick, where water bubbles will appear with the oil. A newly developed method of testing for coolant leaks is to pour a water-soluble dye into the radiator. The dye contains a fluorescent powder which turns green when exposed to a special test lamp's rays.

TESTING FOR AN EXHAUST GAS LEAK
Start the test with a cold engine. Disconnect the fan belt so that the water pump does not operate. Disconnect the upper hose at the radiator. Drain the system until the water level is even with the top of the block. Remove the thermostat and re-

The source of water leaks can also be pinpointed by the use of a special fluorescent powder that can be added to the coolant. A blacklight is used to pick up the leak.

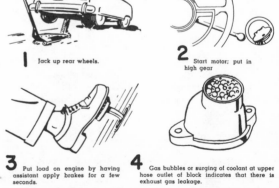

1 Jack up rear wheels.

2 Start motor; put in high gear

3 Put load on engine by having assistant apply brakes for a few seconds.

4 Gas bubbles or surging of coolant at upper hose outlet of block indicates that there is exhaust gas leakage.

To test for a crack in the block or head, which lets hot exhaust gases pass through the coolant, place a load on the engine and check for exhaust bubbles at the top water hose casting.

To check a cooling system for leaks, it can be pressurized by this special pump, and then the gauge can be checked to see whether the system holds the pressure.

A defective seal in the pressure cap (black arrow) will prevent the system from building up pressure.

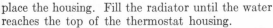

place the housing. Fill the radiator until the water reaches the top of the thermostat housing.

The object of this test is to place a load on the engine so that combustion chamber pressures approach maximum to force hot exhaust gases through any small leak that might exist.

To load the engine: jack up the rear wheels, start the engine, place the shift lever in high gear, open the accelerator wide with your right foot; at the same time apply the foot brakes with your left foot to hold the engine speed to about 20 mph road speed.

Gas bubbles or surging at the upper outlet indicate that exhaust gas is leaking into the cooling system. The test must be conducted quickly to prevent the coolant from boiling in the head.

Another method of testing the engine for leaks is to use a special radiator pressure pump. Drain some water until the level is about ½" below the radiator neck. Attach the tester and apply 15 psi pressure. If the pressure drops, check all points

for an exterior leak. (Use 15 psi pressure only on cars with a 14 psi cap.)

If you cannot locate an exterior leak after the gauge shows a drop in pressure, detach the tester and run the engine to normalize it. Reattach the tester and pump it to 7 psi while the engine is running. Race the engine and, if the dial fluctuates, it indicates a combustion leak. *CAUTION: Pressure builds up fast!* Never let the pressure exceed 15 psi. Release excess pressure immediately!

On V-8 engines, detach the wires from one bank of spark plugs. Operate the engine on the other bank. If the needle continues to fluctuate, it indicates that the leak is in the bank still in operation. If the needle ceases to fluctuate, the leak is in the other bank.

A lean fuel mixture will cause excessively high combustion chamber temperatures, which generally result in spark plug and valve burning.

The same tester is designed to test the valve in the pressure cap.

COOLING SYSTEM TROUBLESHOOTING CHART

TROUBLES & CAUSES

1. **Overheating**
   - 1a. Insufficient coolant
   - 1b. Rust and scale formations in cooling system
   - 1c. Fan belt slipping
   - 1d. Defective water pump
   - 1e. Rusted-out distributor tube
   - 1f. Radiator or hoses clogged
   - 1g. Radiator air flow restricted
   - 1h. Thermostat stuck closed
2. **Engine fails to reach normal operating temperature**
   - 2a. Thermostat defective
   - 2b. Temperature sending unit defective
   - 2c. Temperature indicator defective
3. **Slow warm-up**
   - 3a. Thermostat defective
   - 3b. Manifold heat control stuck open
   - 3c. Automatic choke not closing properly
4. **Loss of coolant**
   - 4a. Leaking radiator
   - 4b. Loose or damaged hose connections
   - 4c. Defective water pump
   - 4d. Cylinder head gasket defective or loose
   - 4e. Uneven tightening of cylinder head bolts
   - 4f. Cracked block or head
   - 4g. Pressure cap defective

TROUBLESHOOTING THE FUEL SYSTEM

The fuel system furnishes a combustible air-fuel mixture to each cylinder. Failure of the fuel system to function properly can result in various complaints: hard starting, poor performance, and excessive fuel consumption.

HARD STARTING

An engine may not start because of either too much or not enough fuel in the combustion chamber. Too much fuel can be caused by percolation or overchoking. Insufficient fuel may be the result of a defective fuel pump, a restricted line, a porous flexible line, a plugged gas tank vent, or an empty gas tank.

A quick test of the fuel system is to move the throttle back and forth while looking down into the carburetor bore. If fuel is present it will be squirted out into the throat of the carburetor. If overchoking is suspected, the accelerator pedal should be advanced to a wide-open position while the engine is cranked to admit more air. Do not pump the pedal or you will force more liquid fuel into the intake manifold and aggravate the condition.

POOR PERFORMANCE

Loss of power, resulting from defects in the fuel system, is due to an air-fuel mixture that is either too lean or too rich.

Lean Mixture. The most commonly experienced fuel system trouble is a pause or "flat spot" on acceleration. If such a condition exists, check the operation of the accelerating pump system in the carburetor and see that the manifold heat control is operating properly. To check the carburetor, remove the air cleaner and move the throttle back and forth. A stream of fuel should flow from the accelerating jet if the system is functioning properly. If the fuel stream is missing completely, thin, deflected to one side, or merely dribbling out the carburetor must be overhauled.

Another lean condition may result from too little fuel being supplied by the carburetor during the range period of operation. Such a condition gives a feeling of "mushiness" as the throttle is opened gradually; the engine doesn't seem to respond. In severe cases, the engine may backfire through the carburetor.

A lean condition can also result from a weak fuel pump or a restricted gas line. Generally, the engine seems to run out of fuel at a certain road speed when there are defects in the supply line.

Rich Mixture. A rich mixture will also cause a loss of power. Excessive quantities of fuel will not vaporize and burn completely. Liquid fuels wash the lubricant from the cylinder walls, allowing the rings to make metal-to-metal contact. Scuffed rings and excessive oil and fuel consumption result. The same abusive conditions occur in an engine in which the manifold heat control valve is inoperative. If it is frozen in the open position, unvaporized gasoline will destroy the upper cylinder wall lubrication, resulting in destructive wear. If it is frozen in the closed position, the inducted mixture will be too hot, resulting in a loss of volumetric efficiency and detonation.

A rich mixture may result from high fuel pump pressure which forces the carburetor needle valve off its seat, causing flooding. It also can result from defects in the automatic choke.

FUEL SYSTEM TROUBLESHOOTING CHART

TROUBLES & CAUSES

1. **Mixture too lean**
   - 1a. Manifold air leaks
   - 1b. Defective fuel pump
   - 1c. Defective carburetor
   - 1d. Clogged fuel line
   - 1e. Clogged fuel filter
   - 1f. Flexible gas line leaking
   - 1g. Plugged tank vent
2. **Mixture too rich**
   - 2a. Defective carburetor
   - 2b. Defective automatic choke
   - 2c. Carburetor percolating
   - 2d. Fuel pump pressure too high
3. **No fuel in carburetor**
   - 3a. Gas tank empty
   - 3b. Fuel pump defective
   - 3c. Clogged fuel filter

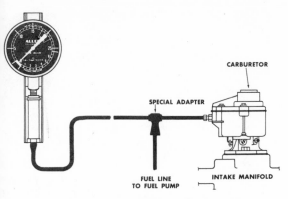

A pressure gauge can be hooked into the fuel line with a "T" fitting to test the pump operating pressure.

3d. Vapor lock
3e. Air leak at fuel pump inlet fitting or porous flexible hose
3f. Fuel line kinked or plugged
3g. Fuel vent closed
3h. Carburetor needle valve stuck in seat by gum

TESTING THE FUEL PUMP

A fuel pump must be tested for both capacity and pressure. The pressure test is made to check for excessively low or high pressures. Low pressure indicates that the pump stroke is relatively short—an indication of worn linkage. High pressure can only be caused by installing the wrong pump or the wrong pump pressure spring during rebuilding. High pressure causes the float bowl level to rise, which enriches the mixture proportionately. In some cases, high pressure forces the needle valve off its seat and causes the carburetor to flood.

Pressure Test. To make the pressure test, disconnect the line leading into the carburetor. Use the proper fitting and a "T" adapter to connect

the gauge into the line. Start the engine and let it idle. A good average pressure is from 3–5 psi.

Capacity Test. The capacity test determines the ability of the pump to produce a specified quantity of fuel in a given time. To make this test, disconnect the rubber hose from the tester and insert it in a pint container. Start the engine and measure the time required to pump 1 pint of fuel. Most standard size pumps will deliver 1 pint in 60 sec; the larger pumps will deliver a pint in 45 sec.

Road Test. A good quick road test of the efficiency of the fuel system is to run the car at high speed while keeping the shift lever in second gear. A good fuel pump will permit the car to attain speeds up to and above 50 mph in second gear. A defective fuel pump will permit the car to attain a high speed but then it will slow down rapidly.

The test results should not be confused with similar results obtained with a defective ignition system which will allow the car to attain a critical speed, and will maintain it regardless of additional throttle pressure, while a defective fuel pump will cause the car to slow down rapidly after the carburetor runs out of fuel.

FUEL PUMP TROUBLESHOOTING CHART

TROUBLES & CAUSES

1. **Insufficient fuel**
   1a. Worn diaphragm
   1b. Worn linkage
   1c. Valves not seating properly
   1d. Clogged fuel screen
   1e. Air leak at sediment bowl, at flexible line, or at inlet connection
   1f. Clogged fuel tank vent
   1g. Clogged fuel line
   1h. Vapor lock
2. **Excessive fuel**
   2a. Wrong diaphragm spring
   2b. Wrong linkage

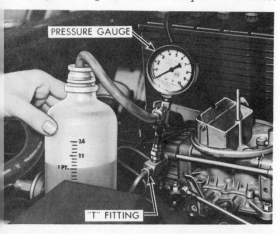

By opening the valve in the "T" fitting, some of the fuel can be diverted into a measuring container. A good pump should deliver about 1 pint of fuel per minute.

A crack in the fuel pump diaphragm allows fuel to leak into the crankcase.

TROUBLESHOOTING THE CARBURETOR

The air-fuel mixture can be measured accurately by means of a combustion analyzer. Actual gas mileage or fuel consumption can be measured by use of a gas-mileage tester. However, there are times when a mechanic will want to make some simple tests to determine the carburetor condition without hooking up elaborate equipment. A rather simple test for the range condition is to advance the throttle to a road speed of about 30 mph. Hold the palm of your hand partially over the choke bore to restrict some of the incoming air. At this speed, a normal carburetor mixture should be somewhat on the lean side. By restricting some of the air, you will enrich the mixture and the engine should speed up *slightly*. If it speeds up considerably, the mixture is too lean; if it doesn't speed up at all, the mixture is too rich. In either case, the carburetor needs to be overhauled.

COMBUSTION ANALYZER

The fact that different gases possess different rates of heat conductivity is the basis of the construction of a combustion analyzer. A rich fuel mixture conducts heat at a different rate than does a lean mixture. Therefore, it becomes a simple matter of measuring the resistance of a heated conductor exposed to air and comparing its resistance with a like heated conductor exposed to the exhaust gas. The resistance is measured by means of a Wheatstone Bridge which responds to any small change in resistance caused by the thermal conductivity of the gas.

To Hook Up a Combustion Analyzer. For accurate analysis, hook up a vacuum gauge and tachometer to the engine in addition to the combustion analyzer. Then run the engine for 15 min. to warm it to operating temperature. Install the sampling unit into the tailpipe of the vehicle and plug the cable into the combustion analyzer panel.

The combustion analyzer needle must be adjusted to the "set" line before starting the test.

To adjust the instrument, turn the SELECTOR switch to the SET position. Turn the SET ADJUST knob until the meter pointer rests on the SET line. Then turn the SELECTOR switch to the TEST position. The instrument is now indicating the air-fuel ratio.

Idling Mixture. Adjust the idle speed to specifications. The analyzer should read between 11.5 and 13.0 on the air-fuel meter with the vacuum gauge reading between 18″ and 22″ Hg. If the reading does not fall between these limits, adjust the idle mixture screw until it does. If you cannot obtain a satisfactory reading or if you have to bottom the adjusting screw to obtain the correct air-fuel mixture, the carburetor should be overhauled.

Accelerating Mixture. Run the engine at a speed of 2000 rpm. Open the throttle fully and immediately snap it shut before the engine picks up too much speed. The meter pointer should move toward the rich side. If it moves to the right, or doesn't move at all, the accelerating circuit is too lean for good performance. The carburetor should be overhauled.

High Speed Mixture. Road test the car with the equipment hooked up in the front compartment. With the engine running at 2000 rpm, the analyzer meter should read between 12.5 and 14.5. If it doesn't, the carburetor should be repaired.

All analyzers are accurate within the normal range of operating mixtures. However, they are not accurate on ratios above 14.7/1.0 because so much air is added to the fuel that free oxygen is

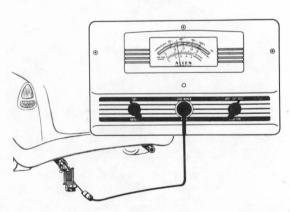

A combustion analyzer is attached to the tail pipe to provide an accurate analysis of the air-fuel ratio passing through the engine.

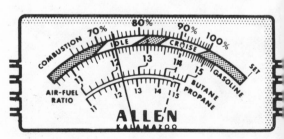

The needle will read the mixture after the exhaust gases pass through it. In this case, the idle is correctly adjusted at 12–1.

A vacuum gauge is very useful to adjust and balance dual carburetors. The mixture is adjusted correctly when the vacuum gauge reads at its highest point.

A tachometer is another essential instrument to assist you in adjusting the idle speed to specifications.

sent through the engine, which reverses the thermal conductivity of the gas, and, therefore, the meter will read rich. If extreme leanness is suspected, and the meter reads rich, the analyzer can be checked for a reversed reading by partially choking the carburetor with the palm of your hand. If the meter needle continues toward the rich side, the meter is reading correctly. If the needle swings first to the lean side and then back to the rich side, the original reading was in error and the air-fuel ratio is leaner than 14.7/1.0.

GAS MILEAGE TESTER

A fuel-measuring device, composed of a graduated tube holding $\frac{1}{10}$ gal. of gasoline between indicating lines, is the basis for an accurate gas mileage tester. The instrument is positioned on the passenger-side front door window where it can be observed. This instrument is invaluable in showing a heavy-footed driver where his gasoline goes. It is a necessary tool to satisfy a gas mileage complaint after a carburetor overhaul.

Two rubber hoses are connected to the fuel pump and carburetor. The tenth of a mile dial on the odometer is used to read the mileage directly because of the $\frac{1}{10}$ of a gallon size of the testing device.

TACHOMETER

Another valuable tool needed by a carburetor mechanic is the tachometer. This electrical meter is connected to the ignition primary terminal of the distributor. It measures the number of times that the primary circuit is interrupted. This information is translated into engine rpm. A tachometer is very useful in balancing dual carburetor adjustments and for setting the idle speed to specifications.

CARBURETOR TROUBLESHOOTING CHART

TROUBLES & CAUSES

1. **Lean condition on range—surges**
   - 1a. Air leaks at manifold or carburetor flange
   - 1b. Clogged bowl vent
   - 1c. Needle valve seat orifice too small
   - 1d. Fuel level too low in bowl
   - 1e. Clogged air bleeds
   - 1f. Wrong main jet or metering rod installed
   - 1g. Clogged main jet
   - 1h. Worn throttle shaft
   - 1i. Insufficient fuel pump pressure or volume
   - 1j. Leaking heat riser
   - 1k. Manifold heat control stuck open
   - 1l. Leaking vacuum lines or defective vacuum booster pump.

2. **Rich condition on range**
   - 2a. Fuel too high in carburetor
   - 2b. Heavy float
   - 2c. Dirt under needle valve
   - 2d. Needle valve orifice too large
   - 2e. High fuel pump pressure
   - 2f. Restricted air cleaner
   - 2g. Wrong metering rod or main jet installed
   - 2h. Power jet leaking

3. **Excessive fuel consumption**
   - 3a. High float level
   - 3b. Heavy float
   - 3c. Worn or dirty float valve and seat
   - 3d. Worn metering rods and jets
   - 3e. Power jet not shutting off in the range
   - 3f. Idle mixture adjustment set too rich
   - 3g. Plugged idle vents
   - 3h. Carbonized throttle bore
   - 3i. Worn throttle shaft
   - 3j. Accelerating pump stroke too long
   - 3k. Worn linkage
   - 3l. Sticking choke valve
   - 3m. High fuel pump pressure
   - 3n. Clogged air cleaner
   - 3o. Fuel bleeding from accelerating pump discharge nozzle

4. Poor acceleration
  4a. Accelerating jet clogged
  4b. Defective accelerating pump plunger
  4c. Incorrect adjustment on pump stroke
  4d. Worn linkage
  4e. Leaking check valve in pump circuit
  4f. Fuel level too low
  4g. Too lean or too rich a range mixture
  4h. Manifold heat control stuck in open position
  4i. Air leaking into manifold
  4j. Carburetor throttle not opening fully
  4k. Choke valve stuck closed
  4l. Power jet not opening

5. Poor idling
  5a. Air leaking into intake manifold
  5b. Incorrect adjustment of idle mixture adjustment screw
  5c. Idle mixture adjustment screw grooved
  5d. Idle speed set too slow
  5e. Float level too high
  5f. Worn throttle shaft
  5g. Leaking vacuum power jet diaphragm
  5h. Carbon formation around the throttle plate
  5i. Dashpot adjustment incorrect
  5j. Automatic choke fast idle linkage not set correctly

6. Poor low-speed performance
  6a. Idle adjusting screws not balanced
  6b. Clogged idle transfer holes
  6c. Restricted idle air bleeds and passages

7. Stalling when accelerator is released suddenly
  7a. Improperly adjusted dashpot
  7b. Defective dashpot
  7c. Clogged air bleeds
  7d. Clogged idle passages
  7e. Leaking intake manifold and/or carburetor gaskets
  7f. Idle speed set too low

8. Hard starting
  8a. Automatic choke not closing properly
  8b. Binding linkage in the choke circuit
  8c. Restricted choke vacuum passages
  8d. Air leaking into the choke vacuum passages

TROUBLESHOOTING THE CHEVROLET CORVETTE FUEL INJECTOR

Before starting to troubleshoot the fuel injection unit, make sure that both the engine and the ignition system have been eliminated as possible sources of trouble.

The commonest difficulty with a fuel injection unit is an air leak. The quickest test for an air leak is to spray each of the signal lines, nozzle blocks, and rubber sleeve connections with water from a pump-type oil can while the engine is idling. If a leak is present, a sucking sound will be heard as the water is drawn in by the vacuum.

To check for leak in the enrichment or main control diaphragm, disconnect the vacuum signal line at the end opposite the diaphragm connection and attach a hose from a manometer with a vacuum source to the tube as shown.

Close the vacuum release valve on the manometer and apply a vacuum to the diaphragm. If the

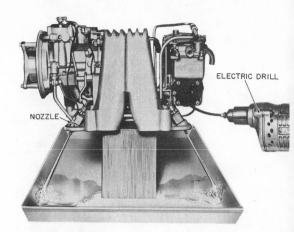

NOZZLE   ELECTRIC DRILL

The fuel injector unit can be tested by filling it with kerosene and driving it with an electric drill in order to inspect the spray pattern. *CAUTION: Don't use gasoline, or arcing at the drill brushes may start a fire!*

diaphragm leaks, the manometer needle will drop slowly back. When testing the main control diaphragm, disconnect the vacuum signal line from the opposite end of the tee and install a plug. If the main control diaphragm leaks, replace the fuel meter; if the enrichment diaphragm leaks, replace the diaphragm.

Never apply a vacuum greater than 4″ Hg to the main control diaphragm, as it may damage the fuel meter. The enrichment diaphragm should be checked by applying 12″–16″ Hg. *CAUTION: It is most important that you do not exceed the specified levels of vacuum, even momentarily, or you will damage the fuel meter irreparably.*

FUEL INJECTOR TROUBLESHOOTING CHART

TROUBLES & CAUSES

1. Engine won't start
  1a. If starting trouble occurs when the engine is hot, check to see that the starting cut-off switch (microswitch) is being actuated by the throttle cam at ¾ throttle. Bend the switch bracket if necessary.
  1b. If the starting solenoid on the fuel meter does not operate when the starter is engaged with the throttle closed, it may be due to a defect in the starting cut-off switch or the solenoid.
  1c. If no fuel is flowing to the fuel distributor, loosen the fuel line at the fuel meter while the engine is cranking. The trouble may be due to a sticking fuel valve.
  1d. To check the fuel line to the fuel distributor, remove one set of nozzles from the nozzle block to see whether fuel flows while cranking the engine. If no fuel flows, the fuel distributor check valve is sticking or the fuel meter-to-distributor line is clogged.
  1e. If fuel flows from the nozzles, check for a large air leak.

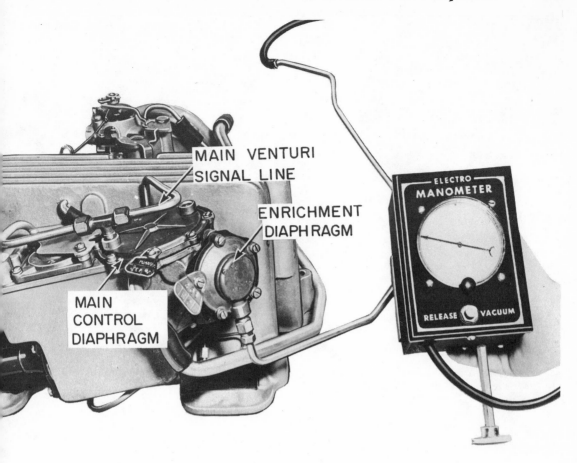

MAIN VENTURI
SIGNAL LINE

ENRICHMENT
DIAPHRAGM

ELECTRO
MANOMETER

RELEASE   VACUUM

MAIN
CONTROL
DIAPHRAGM

The diaphragm of a fuel injector must be tested by means of a manometer and vacuum source.

. Engine starts and dies

2a. This is usually due to residual vapors in the engine. Accelerate the engine several times after starting to purge it. This is especially important in hot weather.

2b. If the engine will not accelerate properly, it may be due to a broken or improperly connected fuel meter pump drive cable. Also it may be due to the enrichment lever not resting on the power (rich) stop when the engine is shut off. After the engine is started, the enrichment lever should remain on the power stop as long as the throttle tab is on the fast idle cam; otherwise, there may be leakage past the enrichment check valve in the cold enrichment housing.

2c. The solenoid should release after the engine starts; otherwise, there may be binding or the wiring is improperly connected.

2d. Check the main control diaphragm vacuum lines for leaks.

2e. If trouble occurs on a cold start, see that the cold enrichment coil cover is indexed properly (1½ notches rich). Check the fast idle cam rod adjustment and see that there is no binding in the linkage. The throttle tab must rest on the stop of the fast idle cam for the first few minutes of engine operation. If the

engine seems to be starving for fuel, disconnect the enrichment line at the cold enrichment housing to provide full enrichment. If this eliminates the trouble, the enrichment valve in the cold enrichment housing is not seating properly. Clean or replace the housing.

2f. The spill plunger may be sticking. It can be moved manually by pushing on the solenoid plunger.

2g. Check for a leak in the main control diaphragm. If the diaphragm leaks, the fuel meter must be replaced.

2h. Check the engine fuel pump for capacity and pressure (5¼–6½ psi).

3. Flat spot

3a. Test for a vacuum leak at the signal lines and fittings.

3b. See that the main control diaphragm venturi signal passage in the air meter is clean and that the auxiliary signal passages are open.

3c. Be sure that the restriction in the main control diaphragm tee is open.

3d. Test the main control diaphragm for leaks.

3e. The spill plunger may be sticking.

3f. The enrichment diaphragm may be leaking.

3g. Check the enrichment control diaphragm rod length which should allow proper cut-in for power and economy.

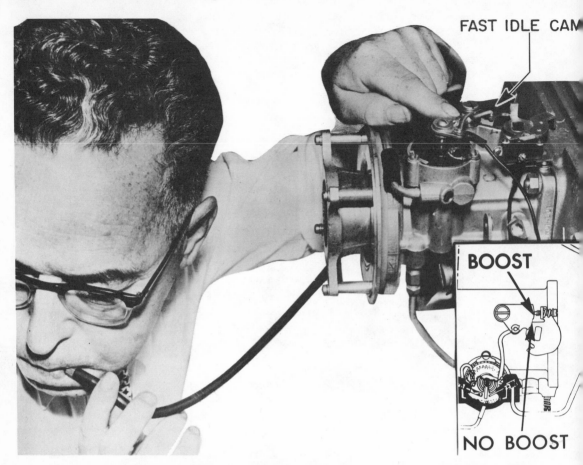

To check the cold enrichment rod length adjustment, blow into a rubber hose connected to the tube coming from the housing. If the choke rod length is correct, a slight air leak should be heard. Repeat with the throttle tab on the second step of the fast idle cam, where no air leak should be heard. Bend the rod to lengthen or shorten it to meet the above requirements.

3h. Test to be sure that the enrichment diaphragm is receiving vacuum from the cold enrichment housing. If not, the trouble may be a broken heat element post, burned-out heat element, or a stuck ball in the enrichment valve.

4. Surge

4a. Check the engine fuel pump and the ignition system, especially the spark plugs, for proper operation. See that the ignition timing is set correctly.

4b. Inspect the fuel filter in the fuel supply line to see that it is not obstructed.

4c. Test for leaks at the vacuum signal lines.

4d. If surging seems to result from an overrich mixture, check the enrichment control diaphragm for leaks. If surging is caused by a lean mixture, test the main control diaphragm for leaks.

4e. See that the spill plunger is operating freely.

5. Rough idle

5a. Adjust the ignition timing, the idle speed, and the idle mixture adjustment.

5b. If the idle fuel adjusting screw has little or no effect on the operation of the engine, the spill plunger may be sticking.

5c. There must be no perceptible vacuum signal from the boost tube at the cold enrichment housing when the rubber sleeve is disconnected and your finger is placed over the tube. Make this test when the throttle tab is off the fast idle cam.

5d. There may be a leak in the signal lines.

5e. Test for a plugged nozzle by shorting out one spark plug at a time.

5f. The enrichment lever must leave the economy stop at 9″ Hg or below and arrive at the power stop at 3″ Hg or above.

5g. Test for vacuum leaks, especially around the nozzle blocks and vent tubes. See that the small gasket is properly seated on each nozzle.

5h. Check for obstructions in the nozzle block vent tubes.

6. Poor fuel economy

6a. Be sure that the enrichment lever rests on the economy stop after the normal warm-up period.

6b. After the engine is warmed up, disconnect the rubber sleeve of the signal boost tube and hold your finger over the tube to see if there is any vacuum signal passing the signal boost valve.

in the cold enrichment housing.

6c. Test to be sure that accurate manifold vacuum signals are reaching the enrichment diaphragm. Make a vacuum check on the engine manifold and another at the enrichment signal line connection at the cold enrichment housing. The readings should not vary over 1" Hg; otherwise, there is a partially closed enrichment valve in the cold enrichment housing, or a leaking gasket between the housing and the air meter.

6d. Test for an enrichment diaphragm leak.

6e. Visually check to see that the ratio stop screw positions have not been altered. These stops are set at the factory and the locknuts and screws covered with a blue sealer. Replace the fuel meter if these adjustments have been altered.

TROUBLESHOOTING THE ELECTRICAL SYSTEM

The battery is the heart of the electrical system; it supplies the entire system with the current it needs to function. The generator charges the battery and develops the voltage or pressure on which the rest of the electrical system must work. The operation of all units is so interrelated that the improper functioning of any one will generally cause a malfunction in the others. For this reason, it is customary to make a series of tests to determine the condition of the entire electrical system to make sure that all troubles have been uncovered. All authorities recommend that the electrical system be tested in the following order: cranking circuit, charging circuit, and then the ignition circuit. In each case, the battery should be tested first because its condition determines the operating voltage of the entire electrical system of the car, and it is a functional part of each basic circuit.

TROUBLESHOOTING THE BATTERY

Two battery tests are generally performed; one has to do with the chemical condition of the electrolyte, and the second with the capacity of the battery to deliver the necessary quantities of electricity.

The electrolyte test is made with a hydrometer which measures the density of the fluid. As a battery becomes discharged, a chemical reaction takes place in which the heavy sulfuric acid combines with the lead of the plates. As the sulfuric acid leaves the electrolyte, the solution contains more water than acid. This lightens the density, which can be measured by a hydrometer; a reading of 1.270 indicates a fully charged battery, one of 1.175 a battery low in charge.

The second test measures the current-delivering ability of the battery. To make this test, place the battery under a heavy load so that about 200 amperes are flowing. At the same time, check the cell voltage with a low-reading voltmeter. If each

---

PM TUNE-UP WORK SHEET

Name_____ Repair Order No. _____

Address_____

City and State_____ Phone No. _____

Car_____ Year_____ License_____ Miles_____

REGULAR CHECK UP	( )	POOR GAS MILEAGE	( )
ENGINE LOSES POWER	( )	HARD STARTING	( )
ENGINE MISSES	( )	ENGINE DIES	( )

OPERATION NO. 1 — **BATTERY AND STARTER**
1. Starter Test: Spec. _____ Volts. Reads _____ Volts.
2. Battery Load Test: Spec. _____ Volts. Reads _____ Volts.
3. Clean top of battery and hold down.
4. Clean, tighten and lubricate battery cable terminals.

Additional Repairs or Adjustments Needed: _____ No _____ Yes (see recommendations).

OPERATION NO. 2 — **COMPRESSION AND SPARK PLUGS**
1. Compression readings: (1 2 3 4 5 6 7 8)
   ( ) OK ( ) Mechanical corrections necessary.
2. Spark Plugs: _____ OK _____ Not OK _____ Cleaned.

Additional Repairs or Adjustments Needed: _____ No _____ Yes (see recommendations).

OPERATION NO. 3 — **ELECTRICAL AND MECHANICAL DISTRIBUTOR CHECK**
1. Check Cam Angle Variation.
2. Check manual and vacuum spark advance, and adjust.
3. Replace contact points, and condenser.
4. Replace breaker plate, is necessary.
5. Test condenser.
6. Test ignition coil.
7. Adjust cam angle.

Additional Repairs or Adjustments Needed: _____ No _____ Yes (see recommendations).

OPERATION NO. 4 — **SECONDARY IGNITION**
1. Secondary Ignition Voltage: Spec. _____ Reads _____
2. Secondary Current Spec.: (1 2 3 4 5 6 7 8) Reads
3. Check and set initial timing.
4. Clean and tighten High Tension wiring connections.

Additional Repairs or Adjustments Needed: _____ No _____ Yes (see recommendations).

OPERATION NO. 5 — **CARBURETION**
1. Clean air cleaner.
2. Set carburetor idle mixture screws to manufacturer's spec.
3. Set engine idle speed to manufacturer's spec.
4. Readjust idle mixture screws to obtain highest engine vacuum. (Highest vacuum should be obtained with mixture screws within number of turns recommended by vehicle manufacturer.)
5. Check air-fuel ratio: _____ OK _____ No

Additional Repairs or Adjustments Needed: _____ No _____ Yes (see recommendations).

OPERATION NO. 6 — **CHARGING SYSTEM**
1. Check Generator.
2. Check voltage regulator setting.
3. Check current regulator setting.
4. Check cutout relay closing voltage.

Additional Repairs or Adjustments Needed: _____ No _____ Yes (see recommendations).

A typical tune-up worksheet which is used to make sure that no vital test has been missed.

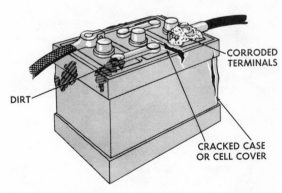

CORRODED TERMINALS

DIRT

CRACKED CASE OR CELL COVER

A visual inspection is often helpful in discovering battery defects.

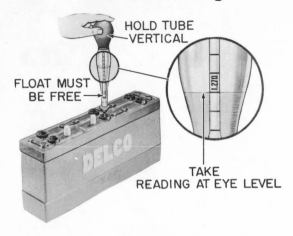

HOLD TUBE VERTICAL

FLOAT MUST BE FREE

TAKE READING AT EYE LEVEL

A hydrometer is used to measure the specific gravity of the electrolyte.

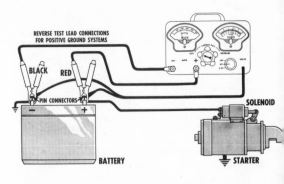

REVERSE TEST LEAD CONNECTIONS FOR POSITIVE GROUND SYSTEMS

BLACK   RED

PIN CONNECTORS

BATTERY

SOLENOID

STARTER

These are the connections that must be made to tes the battery under load.

cell drops below 1.5 volts, the battery condition is low. If the voltage of an individual cell drops below the others, by 0.15 volt, a defect is indicated in that cell. A shorted separator will cause the voltage of a cell to drop to zero, and the needle may even reverse itself.

Such a high-rate test should not be performed on a discharged battery—one with a specific gravity reading of 1.225 or less; otherwise, the battery may be damaged. The load should not be left on over 20 sec. for each cell test, or the plates may be damaged.

Making a Battery Capacity Test. Turn the carbon pile knob to the OFF position. Turn the VOLTS switch to the 16-volt position for testing a 12-volt battery. Connect the test leads as shown.

Turn the carbon pile knob toward the *increase* direction until the ammeter reads 3 times the ampere-hour rating of the battery. At the end of 15 sec. read the voltmeter. If the voltage is

9.0 volts or higher for a 12-volt battery (4.5 volt for a 6-volt battery), the capacity of the battery is good.

Making a Cell Voltage Test. Where the battery voltage drops below 9.0 volts (4.5 for a 6-volt battery) on the load test, each cell should be checked with a low-reading voltmeter.

There are two types of low-reading voltmeter used for testing the condition of battery cells. One type contains a shunt across the prods to place an appropriate load on the cell while the voltage test is being made. The other type has no shunt and, therefore, the starting motor must be operated to load the battery while the voltage is being measured.

Readings are obtained by pressing the prod points firmly into the post or cell connectors of each cell. The meter prods must be reversed a

A battery tester has a carbon pile rheostat to place a load on the battery for testing its capacity.

Some cell testors have a shunt (arrow) to place a loa on the cell while the meter measures the voltage.

Meters without a shunt require you to load the battery by operating the starting motor.

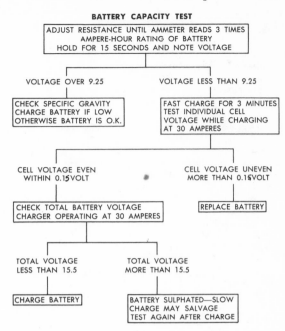

| ADJUST RESISTANCE UNTIL AMMETER READS 3 TIMES AMPERE-HOUR RATING OF BATTERY HOLD FOR 15 SECONDS AND NOTE VOLTAGE |

VOLTAGE OVER 9.25 — CHECK SPECIFIC GRAVITY CHARGE BATTERY IF LOW OTHERWISE BATTERY IS O.K.

VOLTAGE LESS THAN 9.25 — FAST CHARGE FOR 3 MINUTES TEST INDIVIDUAL CELL VOLTAGE WHILE CHARGING AT 30 AMPERES

CELL VOLTAGE EVEN WITHIN 0.15 VOLT — CHECK TOTAL BATTERY VOLTAGE CHARGER OPERATING AT 30 AMPERES

CELL VOLTAGE UNEVEN MORE THAN 0.15 VOLT — REPLACE BATTERY

TOTAL VOLTAGE LESS THAN 15.5 — CHARGE BATTERY

TOTAL VOLTAGE MORE THAN 15.5 — BATTERY SULPHATED—SLOW CHARGE MAY SALVAGE TEST AGAIN AFTER CHARGE

Roadmap for measuring the capacity of the battery under operating conditions.

the meter is moved along to the next cell because each one has reversed polarity. Most batteries are made with buried cell connectors; therefore, the sealing compound must be pierced by the meter prods. After completion of the test, the sealing compound must be pressed back into place. It can be resealed with a hot soldering copper.

Making a 3-Minute Battery Charge Test. If the capacity load test indicates that the battery condition is not up to specifications, a 3-min. charge test should be made. This test measures the voltage of each cell after the battery has been on charge 3 min. It is an excellent indication of the battery plate condition.

Turn the battery selector switch to 16 volts for a 12-volt battery (or to 8 for a 6-volt battery) and connect the fast-rate charger to the battery (red clips to the positive terminal and black to the negative). The voltmeter should now be connected. However, care must be taken that the voltmeter clips contact the battery terminal posts and not the charger clips. Turn the charger on and set the time switch beyond 3 min. and then back to exactly 3 min. Adjust the charging rate to 40 amp. for a 12-volt battery (75 amp. for a 6-volt battery).

After 3 min. when the time switch has returned the charger to a slow-charge rate, reset the switch to a fast-charging rate. Note the voltmeter reading which should not exceed 15.5 volts (7.75 on a 6-volt battery): otherwise, the battery is sulfated and should be replaced.

If the voltage is within satisfactory limits, proceed to test each cell by setting the voltmeter to the 4-volt scale. With the charger operating on fast charge, measure the voltage across each cell. If the readings vary by more than 0.15 volt, the battery should be replaced.

If the battery capacity test indicated low, but the cell voltage readings were even, but low, the state of the battery charge is low, and it should be recharged.

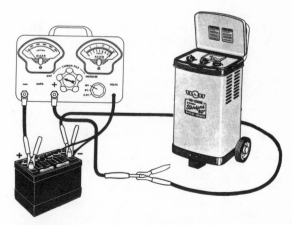

Connections for the fast-rate charger required in the previous test.

BATTERY TROUBLESHOOTING CHART

TROUBLES & CAUSES

1. **Low specific gravity readings**
   1a. Low state of charge
   1b. Loss of acid through leaks
   1c. Acid absorbed by spongy plates
   1d. Sulfated plates
   1e. Electrical drain due to acid resistance path on top of the case or to a short circuit in the car wiring
2. **Low individual cell voltage readings**
   2a. Low state of charge
   2b. Loss of acid through a leak
   2c. Shorted plates caused by a defective separator
3. **Low current capacity**
   3a. Low state of charge
   3b. Sulfated plates
   3c. Low fluid level
   3d. Acid absorbed by spongy plates
   3e. Powdered-out positive plates from overcharging
   3f. Replacement battery too small for vehicle demands

TROUBLESHOOTING THE CRANKING SYSTEM

The condition of the cranking system has a decided effect on the ease of starting the engine—or the lack of it. A good cranking system will spin the engine fast enough to draw in a full combustible charge, compress it high enough to develop sufficient heat to dry out most of the wet fuel particles, and maintain a sufficiently high battery voltage so that the ignition system can operate efficiently.

Any defect in the cranking circuit slows down the cranking speed. And, because the starting motor fields and armature are connected in series, a slower speed allows more time for the current to flow through each armature coil which increases the current drain on the system. In turn, this lowers the battery voltage available to the ignition system which then operates at less than maximum efficiency. Thus, a vicious cycle is set up which results in a hard starting complaint.

Making a Starting Motor Current Draw Test. Excessive starting motor current draw is a certain indication of trouble in the starting motor circuit, *provided that the cranking load is normal.* A rebuilt engine or extremely cold weather causes an excessively heavy load on the starting motor, and it will draw more current.

To make a starting motor current draw test, connect the test meters to the circuits as shown. Turn the selector switch to 16 volts (8 volts for a 6-volt battery). Connect a jumper lead from the primary terminal of the distributor to ground to prevent the engine from starting.

Crank the engine and note the *exact* voltage indicated on the voltmeter. Now, without cranking the engine, turn the control knob of the tester clockwise until the voltmeter reads exactly the

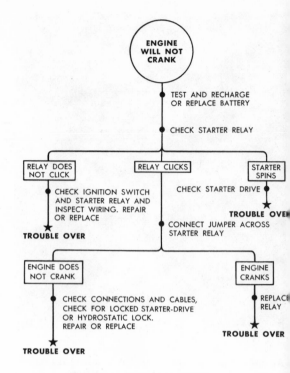

Roadmap for troubleshooting a starting motor that does not crank the engine.

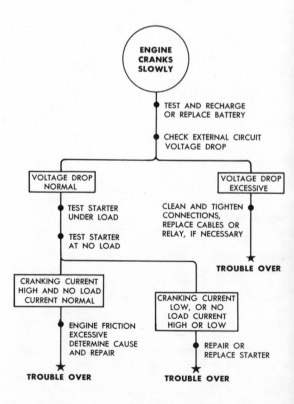

Roadmap for troubleshooting a starting motor that cranks the engine too slowly.

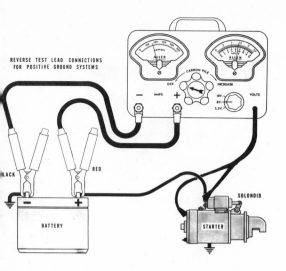

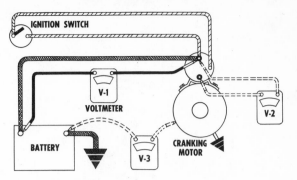

To measure the voltage drop across parts of the starting motor circuit, and to isolate resistance connections, move the meters to the positions shown.

Correct way to hook up the meters to measure the starting motor current draw.

same as it did in the previous test when the starter was being operated. The ammeter will now read the current draw, which should be between 150 to 210 amp. depending on the type of starting motor. Readings in excess of specifications indicate that the starting motor should be removed for repair.

Making a Starting Motor Cable Resistance Test. Resistance between terminals is a common cause of starting difficulties. Resistance cuts down the amount of current flowing to the starting motor and the voltage to the ignition system. The starting motor cranks the engine more slowly and the ignition system functions inefficiently. Therefore, this is one of the more important tests in troubleshooting.

Turn the voltmeter selector switch to the 4-volt position and connect the test leads as shown. (The

meter will read off-scale until the engine is cranked.) The voltmeter leads must contact the battery posts rather than the cable connectors. Ground the ignition primary lead to prevent the engine from starting.

Crank the engine and observe the voltmeter reading. The voltage loss should not exceed 0.4 volt for Delco-Remy and Ford systems, and 0.3 volt for an Autolite system. If a higher reading is registered, the voltmeter leads should be connected across each switch in turn until the high-resistance connection is located. The maximum voltage drop across any connection should be 0.0 volt; across each switch, 0.1 volt; and across each cable, 0.2 volt. If any connection exceeds these readings, it should be taken apart and cleaned. Any switch exceeding the specified voltage drop should be replaced.

CRANKING SYSTEM TROUBLESHOOTING CHART

TROUBLES & CAUSES

1. **Cranks engine slowly**
   1a. Low state of battery charge
   1b. High resistance battery cable connection
   1c. High resistance starter switch
   1d. Bent armature shaft
   1e. Worn bushing in the drive end
   1f. Dirty or worn commutator
   1g. Worn brushes or weak brush springs
2. **Doesn't crank the engine at all**
   2a. Dead battery
   2b. Broken battery cable or high resistance connection
   2c. Open circuit in the ignition-to-solenoid circuit (neutral-safety switch)
   2d. Open circuit in the starting switch
   2e. Open circuit in the starting motor
   2f. Starting motor drive stuck to the flywheel gear
   2g. Hydrostatic lock
3. **Spins, but does not crank the engine**
   3a. Defective starter drive

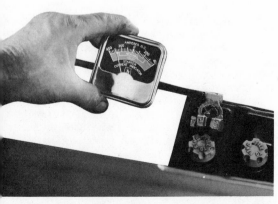

This ammeter is designed to be placed over the battery cable to measure the current draw.

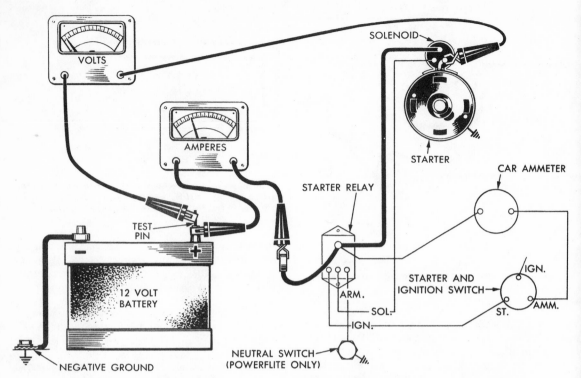

This is another method of testing the voltage drop of the starting motor circuit. With the meters connected as shown, operate the starting motor, and the voltage drop should not exceed 0.2 volt per 100 amp.

TROUBLESHOOTING THE CHARGING SYSTEM

Modern automotive charging systems have a regulator to control the output of the generator or alternator. In practice, the charging rate increases when the battery is discharged and decreases when it is charged. The charging rate may be cut down to a very low rate with a fully charged battery.

To test the charging system, crank the engine with the ignition switch off in order to discharge the battery slightly. (On cars with an ignition key-type starter switch, it may be necessary to remove the coil high tension wire from the center of the distributor cap to prevent the engine from starting.) Now, start the engine and note the charging rate. (On a car without an ammeter, it is necessary to insert an ammeter in the charging circuit.) As the engine is run for a short period, the charging rate should decrease with a properly operating regulator. If the ammeter does not show any charge after the above test, it is an indication that either the generator or the regulator is at fault.

To isolate the trouble on a generator charging system, disconnect the "F" lead from the terminal on the regulator and connect it to a good ground. *CAUTION: The previously used jumper-to-ground wire method should not be used on late-model,*

double-contact, Delco-Remy regulators, or it will burn the VR points. On Ford products, this procedure is reversed. Connect a jumper wire from the "A" terminal to the "F" terminal on the generator. If the generator now charges, the trouble is in the regulator. If the generator still does not charge, the trouble is in the generator. In most cases in which the generator is burned out, the regulator will be found to be defective, too.

If the generator output is excessive, the trouble can be caused by the regulator points being welded together or by a short circuit in a field wire. In either case, there is no regulation, and the generator is running wide open. To test for this type of trouble, it must be remembered that there are two basic types of field circuits: one grounded at the regulator and one supplied with current at the regulator. By removing the field wire from the regulator, the generator can be isolated. If the generator still charges with the field wire removed, then the ground or short is in the generator itself.

Another generator check can be made by removing the cover band. If the inner surface of the band is covered with a layer of solder, the generator was overloaded until the solder from the armature commutator slots melted. Obviously, this leads to open circuited coils in the armature. The wires can be resoldered and the commutator turned, provided that the coils have not grounded out.

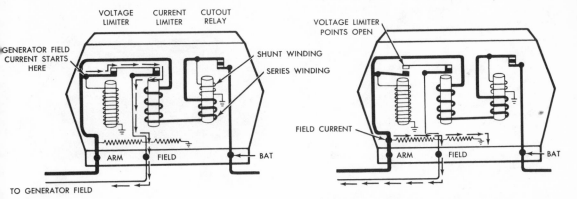

FIELD CURRENT (POINTS CLOSED)

VOLTAGE LIMITER | CURRENT LIMITER | CUTOUT RELAY

GENERATOR FIELD CURRENT STARTS HERE

SHUNT WINDING
SERIES WINDING

ARM | FIELD | ← BAT

TO GENERATOR FIELD

FIELD CURRENT (POINTS OPEN)

VOLTAGE LIMITER POINTS OPEN

FIELD CURRENT

ARM | FIELD | BAT

The regulator controls the output of the generator by varying the strength of its field. When the VR points open (right view) due to increased voltage, the field strength is reduced, thus reducing the generator output.

Otherwise, the armature should be replaced.

Voltage losses, due to poor connections, cause an increase of operating voltage because the generator tries to overcome the added resistance of the circuit by forcing current through at a higher voltage. When the voltage increases, the regulator senses it and returns it to normal by regulating the field. Thus, even though the battery is low in charge, the generator output remains low, and another vicious cycle is set up.

Checking the Voltage Regulator Setting. Turn the test selector to the VOLTAGE REGULATOR position and set the voltage selector for 20 volts (10 volts for a 6-volt system). Turn the voltage selector switch to the side corresponding to the polarity of the car battery. Make the connections as shown.

Turn off all lights and accessories. Operate the engine for at least 15 min. at about 1600 rpm to bring the regulator to operating temperature. Keep the cover in place for all tests.

Reduce the generator output by slowing down the engine to allow the cutout points to open. Now, increase the engine speed until a maximum reading is obtained on the voltmeter. You can tell when the VR points begin to operate by the vibration of the meter needle. Compare the results with the manufacturer's specifications. For the purpose of troubleshooting, you will find that a reading close to 15 volts for a 12-volt system (7.5 volts for a 6-volt system) indicates normal operation of the charging circuit.

If you are using a separate voltmeter and ammeter, it may be necessary to insert a $\frac{1}{4}$ ohm resistor into the line to insure that the battery voltage will rise to the regulator setting. It is pos-

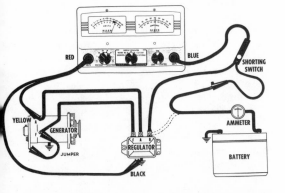

To isolate trouble in the charging circuit, short out the regulator by connecting a jumper between the field terminal and the ground. If the generator now charges, the trouble is in the regulator. This circuit jumper is used only when the generator field wire is internally connected to the main brush. In the other circuit, where the field wire is internally grounded, the jumper must be placed between the field and armature terminals.

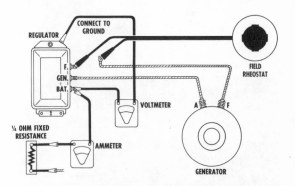

On high-output, double-contact, Delco-Remy regulators, a field rheostat must be connected into the field circuit, or the wire to the field terminal can be disconnected and grounded. If the jumper used in previous tests is connected to ground the field terminal, without disconnecting the wire, the VR points will burn.

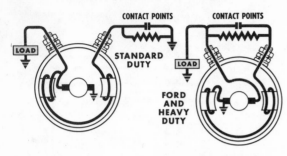

There are two basic types of field circuits, one being grounded through the regulator (left), and the other being grounded inside the generator (right).

A rough commutator surface is a sure indication of trouble in the making.

sible for a battery to be sufficiently undercharged that the regulator setting cannot be reached. The ¼ ohm resistor approximates the resistance of a fully charged battery. The test equipment described above contains such a resistor; it is switched into the circuit automatically whenever the selector switch is set to the VOLTAGE REGULATOR position.

Checking the Current Regulator Setting. Turn the selector knob to the CURRENT REGULATOR position. Make the connections as shown. The regulator must be at operating temperature and the cover must be in place. The voltage regulator must be made inoperative for this test by connecting a jumper as shown.

Cycle the generator by reducing the engine speed to idle in order to permit the cutout points to open, and then increase the engine speed to 2000 rpm. Turn the knob of the LOAD CONTROL to get the highest ammeter reading. This is the setting to which the current regulator is set. Compare it with the manufacturer's specifications. For the

purpose of troubleshooting, a 30-amp. reading is normal for a standard model car. Higher-priced models, with added electrical accessories, and cars with air conditioners require higher-output generators; these should read close to 35 amp.—some as much as 40 amp.

Checking the Voltage Drop in the Charging Circuit. To determine whether loose or corroded connections are causing an undercharged condition of the battery, it is necessary to make a resistance check of the circuit. To do this, adjust the engine speed until the generator charges 20 amp., according to a test ammeter. A voltmeter is connected across the entire charging circuit to measure the voltage drop. By setting the output to exactly 20 amp., an established voltage drop across a normal circuit can be determined and used as the basis for comparison.

To connect the tester into the circuit, turn the test selector to the GENERATOR position, and the voltage selector to the 10-volt position according to battery polarity. Make the connections as shown.

Operate the engine at a speed so that the generator charges exactly 20 amp. according to the test ammeter. Then press the shorting switch button to eliminate the voltage drop in the leads. The voltmeter should read less than 0.75 volt.

To isolate a high-resistance connection, one meter test lead can be moved back in the circuit from terminal to terminal until the defective connection is located by a high reading.

CHARGING SYSTEM TROUBLESHOOTING CHART

TROUBLES & CAUSES

1. Battery requires water too frequently
    1a. Voltage regulator unit set too high
    1b. Current regulator unit set too high
    1c. Cracked battery case

An armature cover band with solder is a sure indication that the armature coils are open circuited.

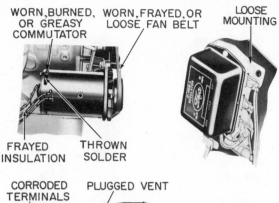

WORN, BURNED, WORN, FRAYED, OR LOOSE
OR GREASY LOOSE FAN BELT MOUNTING
COMMUTATOR

FRAYED THROWN
INSULATION SOLDER

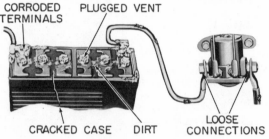

CORRODED PLUGGED VENT
TERMINALS

CRACKED CASE DIRT LOOSE
CONNECTIONS

Visual inspection often uncovers many charging circuit defects.

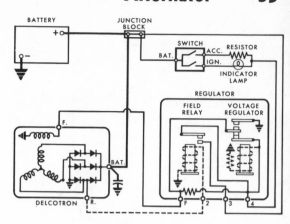

Typical alternator wiring diagram, showing internal circuits.

8c. Cutout relay closing voltage set too low
9. **Noises**
    9a. Bad bearings
    9b. Loose generator drive pulley
    9c. Brushes not seating
    9d. Loose fan belt

TROUBLESHOOTING AN ALTERNATOR CHARGING CIRCUIT

A quick test can be made to isolate charging circuit trouble between the alternator and the regulator by disconnecting the field lead from the regulator to the alternator, and then connecting a jumper wire between the field and output terminals on the alternator. *CAUTION: Always disconnect the battery ground cable before doing any work on the alternator as the terminals are always "hot."* If the alternator charges with the jumper in place, but not with the regulator connected, the regulator is at fault. If the alternator does not charge with the jumper in place, the alternator is at fault.

Before any accurate testing is done, certain preliminary tests should be made as follows: make

2. **Battery will not remain charged**
    2a. Voltage regulator unit set too low
    2b. Current regulator unit set too low
    2c. Short circuit in car wiring
    2d. High-resistance connection in charging circuit
    2e. Excessive low-speed driving while operating accessories
    2f. Defective battery
    2g. Defective generator
    2h. Defective regulator
3. **Battery will not accept a charge**
    3a. Sulfated battery
    3b. Open circuit between cells
4. **Generator has no output**
    4a. Defective generator
    4b. Defective regulator
    4c. Grounded or open lead from armature terminal of generator or regulator
    4d. Ground or open circuit in the field lead
    4e. Field or ground wires reversed on generator
5. **Generator output low**
    5a. Slipping fan belt
    5b. Voltage regulator unit set too low
    5c. Current regulator unit set too low
    5d. High resistance in field circuit
    5e. Defective generator
6. **Generator output too high**
    6a. Voltage regulator unit set too high
    6b. Current regulator unit set too high
    6c. Defective regulator
    6d. Ground or short in field lead
7. **Voltage or current regulator points badly burned**
    7a. Shorted generator field windings
    7b. Radio condenser connected to field terminal
8. **Cutout points chatter**
    8a. Generator polarity reversed
    8b. Battery installed in reverse

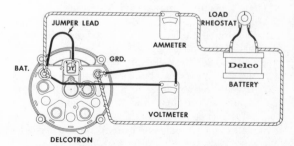

To isolate alternator troubles, a jumper wire should be connected between the field and battery terminals at the alternator, after disconnecting the field wire to the alternator. This test is valid for all manufacturers' products.

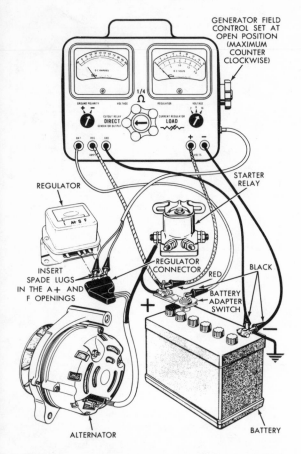

This is the way to hook up a Sun tester to check the output of the alternator. In this case, a Ford system with snap connectors is shown, but this is similar to the other manufacturers' products.

sure that the drive belt is properly tensioned, that the battery is fully charged, and that there are no resistance connections in the charging circuit. Correct any defects before proceeding with the output tests below.

OUTPUT TEST

The alternator output test is made to determine whether the unit is capable of delivering its rated amperage. To make this test, first disconnect the battery ground cable to avoid damaging the unit. Disconnect the field-to-alternator wire, connect a jumper between the field and output terminals so that the field operates at maximum efficiency, and then connect an ammeter in series with the alternator output terminal and the regulator main wire. Connect a voltmeter between the alternator main output terminal and ground, and a carbon-pile rheostat across the battery in order to control the voltage. Hook up the battery ground cable, and then start the engine. Because each manufacturer specifies a different set of test conditions, they are detailed below. Compare the alternator max-

imum output with the rated output as given in the specification tables in the Appendix under each car model.

DELCO-REMY. Start the engine and adjust its speed to 2500 rpm (alternator 6000 rpm). Adjust the carbon-pile rheostat to read 14.0 volts.

FORD. Start the engine and adjust its speed to exactly 2900 rpm. Adjust the carbon-pile rheostat to read 15.0 volts.

AUTOLITE (PRESTOLITE). Start the engine and adjust its speed until the alternator rotates at 4200 rpm. Adjust the carbon-pile rheostat to read 14.2 volts.

CHRYSLER. Start the engine and adjust its speed to exactly 1250 rpm. Adjust the carbon-pile rheostat to read 15.0 volts.

ALTERNATOR TROUBLESHOOTING CHART

1. Alternator fails to charge
    1a. Blown fuse wire in voltage regulator
    1b. Drive belt loose
    1c. Worn bushings and/or slip rings
    1d. Sticking brushes
    1e. Open field circuit
    1f. Open charging circuit
    1g. Open circuit in stator windings
    1h. Open diode(s)

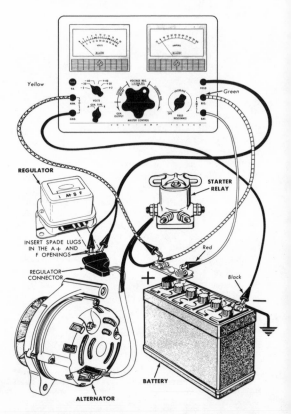

This is the Allen tester hook-up for the same alternator output test. The regulator is out of the circuit, but the field strength can be controlled by the field resistance in the meter.

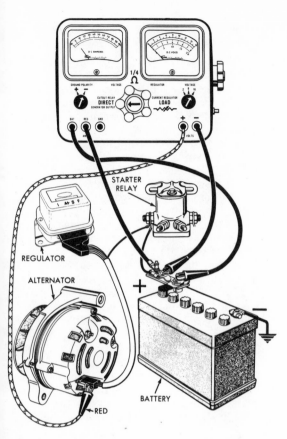

Method of wiring the Sun tester to measure the voltage drop between the alternator and the battery positive terminal.

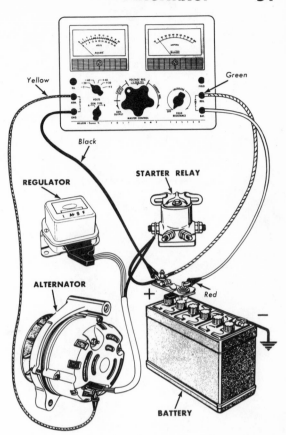

This is the same test as the previous illustration, using Allen test equipment.

2. **Low, unsteady charging rate**
   2a. Loose drive belt
   2b. High resistance at battery terminals
   2c. High resistance in the charging circuit
   2d. High resistance in the ground lead
   2e. Open stator winding
3. **Low output and a low battery**
   3a. High resistance in the charging circuit
   3b. Low regulator setting
   3c. Shorted or open diode
   3d. Grounded stator windings
4. **Excessive charging rate to a fully charged battery**
   4a. Regulator set too high
   4b. Regulator contacts stuck
   4c. Regulator voltage winding open
   4d. Regulator base improperly grounded
5. **Regulator contacts oxidized**
   5a. High regulator setting
   5b. Regulator air gap improperly set
   5c. Shorted rotor field coil windings
6. **Regulator contacts burned**
   6a. High regulator setting
   6b. Shorted rotor field coil windings
7. **Regulator voltage coil windings burned**
   7a. High regulator setting
8. **Regulator contact points stuck**
   8a. Poor ground connection between alternator and regulator

9. **Noisy alternator**
   9a. Alternator mounting loose
   9b. Worn or frayed drive belt
   9c. Worn bearings
   9d. Interference between rotor fan and stator leads or rectifiers
   9e. Rotor or fan damaged
   9f. Open or shorted diode or stator winding
   9g. Loose pulley

TRANSISTOR REGULATOR

A transistor regulator is used to control the alternator output in a manner similar to the conventional relay-type regulator, except that it contains no moving parts. The assembly is composed chiefly of transistors, diodes, resistors, a capacitor, and a thermistor. When the ignition switch is closed, current flows through diode D-1 and transistor TR-1 to the generator field. When the operating voltage reaches the pre-set value, the regulating components cause transistor TR-1 to turn off and on to control the alternator field strength. The thermistor provides temperature compensation. The regulator operating voltage is adjustable in a narrow range by turning the slotted-screw, under the pipe plug, clockwise to decrease the setting. *NOTE: Each notch will change the setting by 0.3 volt.*

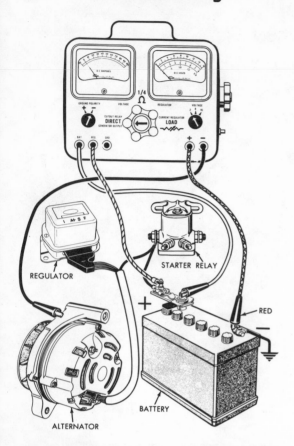

This shows how to hook up a Sun tester to measure the voltage drop between the alternator and battery ground terminals.

TROUBLESHOOTING A TRANSISTOR REGULATOR CHARGING CIRCUIT

Output Test. *CAUTION: Before making any connections to this circuit, temporarily disconnect the battery ground cable to avoid damage to the alternator.* Connect an ammeter in series with the BAT terminal on the alternator and the wire which was connected to this terminal. Connect a voltmeter between the BAT terminal and ground. Disconnect the wiring harness connector from the alternator "F" terminal, and then connect a jumper wire from the alternator "F" terminal to the alternator BAT terminal. This connection removes the regulator from the circuit so that the alternator should charge at its maximum output. Operate the alternator at its specified speed (see Appendix for specifications), turn on accessories, or connect a carbon pile rheostat across the battery to load the system in order to obtain the specified voltage. *CAUTION: Do not allow the alternator to exceed its specified operating voltage or it will be damaged.* Specifications for a typical unit are as follows:

MODEL	VOLTS	AMPERES @ RPM	AMPERES @ RPM
1100648	14.0	32 @ 2000	50 @ 5000

If the output is below specifications, remove and repair the alternator; if it meets specifications, the alternator is in good condition, and the trouble must be in the transistor regulator or associated wiring.

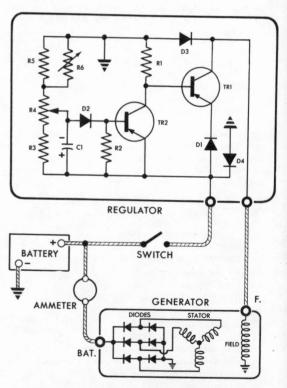

Internal wiring of the alternator and transistorized regulator.

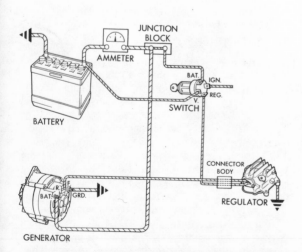

Typical wiring diagram using a transistorized regulator to control the output of the Delco-Remy alternator.

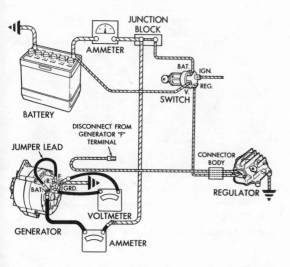

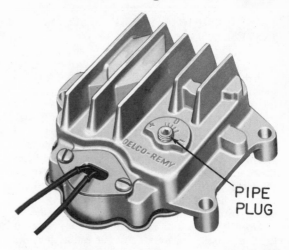

The transistorized regulator has no moving parts. The adjustment for raising or lowering the operating voltage is under the pipe plug.

To test the output of the transistorized charging circuit, use a jumper from the "F" terminal to the battery terminal of the alternator, with the field wire disconnected. This connection is similar to the conventional relay-type regulator jumper connection.

Checking the Voltage Drop. Remove the jumper previously connected, and reconnect the field harness connector to the alternator "F" terminal. Turn on the ignition switch but do not start the engine. Connect a voltmeter positive lead to the battery positive post and the voltmeter negative lead to the regulator positive terminal. Slide the voltmeter prod into the regulator connector body *black* lead terminal to make the connection at the regulator (Part 1). Record the voltage drop. Now, connect the voltmeter positive lead to the regulator mounting bolt and the voltmeter negative lead to the battery negative post (Part 2), and then record the voltage drop. The sum of the two voltage drops must not exceed 0.3 volt, or there

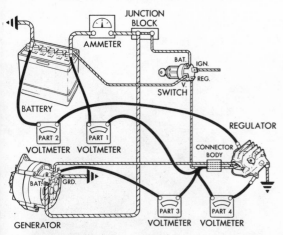

Circuit checks with a voltmeter are used to determine where the trouble is in the transistorized charging circuit. The "part" voltmeter positions are discussed in the text.

is a high resistance connection in the ignition switch or wiring to the regulator.

If the total voltage drop in the previous tests is less than 0.3 volt, continue troubleshooting by connecting the voltmeter positive lead to the regulator positive terminal and the voltmeter negative lead to the alternator "F" terminal. Slide the voltmeter lead prods into the connector body terminal to make the connections (Part 3). If the voltage here is 0.9 volt, the transistor is shorted and the regulator must be replaced. If the voltage here is 2.0 volts or greater, the transistor is open circuited and the regulator must be replaced.

If the voltage at the previous test point (Part 3) is between 0.9 and 2.0 volts, the unit is in good shape and should be adjusted as follows: Operate the engine at approximately 1500 rpm for 10 min. with the headlight lower beams turned on. With the engine running, measure the voltage across the positive terminal and ground by sliding the voltmeter prod into the regulator connector body *black* lead terminal to make the connection (Part 4). Compare the voltage with a typical unit (Model 1116365) as follows: *NOTE: The ambient temperature must be recorded ¼" away from the regulator cover.*

AMBIENT TEMPERATURE				
65°	85°	105°	125°	145°
VOLTAGE SETTING				
13.8–14.5	13.7–14.4	13.5–14.2	13.4–14.1	13.3–14.0

If the voltage is not within limits, the regulator may have to be replaced as there is only a limited adjusting range available. To change the regulator setting, remove the pipe plug on the regulator, insert a small screwdriver to engage the slot of the adjusting screw, and turn the adjustment counterclockwise to increase the setting. *NOTE: Each notch will change the voltage by 0.3 volt.*

TROUBLESHOOTING THE IGNITION SYSTEM

The efficient operation of the ignition system probably has a great deal more to do with the smooth operation of an internal combustion engine than any other mechanical or electrical part. The importance of the ignition system can be realized from the fact that every minute 20,000 sparks are developed and delivered to the spark plugs of an 8-cylinder engine running at high speed. And, that these sparks must be distributed to each of the cylinders when they have been charged with an explosive air-fuel mixture that has been compressed to the point of maximum efficiency. Naturally, any slipup in the chain of events needed to create and time the sparks will result in poor engine performance.

The spark needed to fire the compressed air-fuel mixture is close to 20,000 volts. To step up the battery's 12 volts to the high voltage needed to jump the gaps of the spark plugs is the duty of the ignition coil. This transformer contains a primary and a secondary winding. The primary circuit, operating on the battery voltage, consists of the battery, ignition switch, ignition contact points, condenser, primary winding of the ignition coil, and ballast resistor. The secondary circuit develops the high voltage needed to fire the spark plugs, and it consists of the ignition coil, rotor, distributor cap, high tension wiring, and spark plugs.

The primary circuit contains a set of contact points which interrupts the circuit. The action of interrupting the primary circuit develops the high-tension spark in the secondary circuit. At the same time, the contact-point interruption is precisely timed so as to send the spark to the cylinder at the instant the air-fuel charge has been compressed to the point of maximum efficiency. Naturally, the contact point set must open and close once for each spark delivered, or 20,000 times per minute at top speed. It is no wonder, then, that the contact points require periodic servicing. Without it, they soon deteriorate and cause such troubles as hard starting, misfiring, poor performance, and low fuel mileage.

There is no way to test the performance of the ignition system with accuracy except with precision test equipment. Any other way is subject to error. However, a rough check can be made of the ignition system by road testing the car while placing the engine under a heavy load. Drive the car in high gear at about 6 mph on a smooth road; place your left foot lightly on the brake pedal to put a load on the engine. Open the accelerator fully with your right foot. (Keep from going past the detent in a car with an automatic transmission.) As the engine picks up speed, apply the foot brake to keep the car speed constant at about 25 mph. Ignition troubles will cause the car to

An oscilloscope is frequently used to analyze the ignition system.

jerk sharply. Defective spark plugs are especially sensitive to such a test.

If the car can be driven wide open in second gear, a good ignition system will allow the car to attain a maximum speed. A defective ignition system will cause it to "float" long before it reaches maximum.

USING AN OSCILLOSCOPE TO ANALYZE THE IGNITION SYSTEM

A recent introduction to the field of ignition testing is the oscilloscope. It has long been used by television repairmen to analyze the operation of complex circuitry. The scope "televises" the operation of the entire ignition system, putting the result in pattern form rather than in unit measure by meters, as has been done in the past. The value of the scope as a test instrument depends on the ability of the operator to interpret the meaning of the deviations from the normal wave patterns.

CONNECTING THE SCOPE TO THE ENGINE. Connect one lead of the scope to the main coil wire

Method of hooking the scope to the engine.

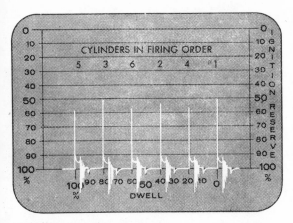

Operating the scope to develop a normal secondary pattern. The six spark indicators are visible for a comparison of their voltages.

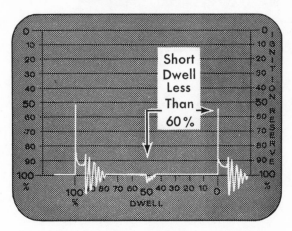

The point of dwell is indicated in per cent.

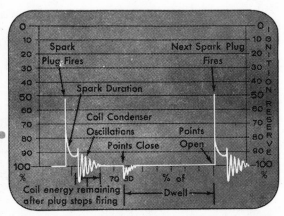

Compressing the pattern to show one cylinder in detail.

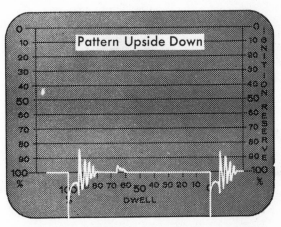

If the pattern is upside down, the coil polarity is reversed.

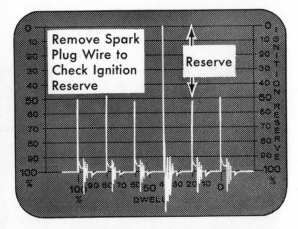

Testing the ignition reserve by removing one spark plug wire. The one peak is the available voltage, and it should be compared with the operating plug voltages to determine just how much reserve is left in the system.

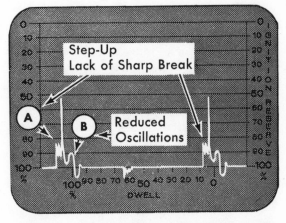

A defective condenser will show these defects in the pattern at "A" and "B."

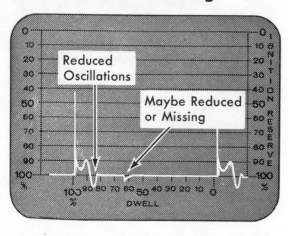

A defective ignition coil will show reduced oscillations.

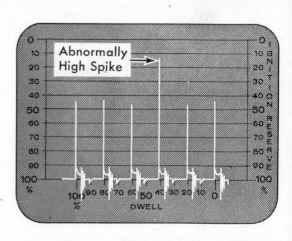

A high spike is an indication of a wide spark plug gap.

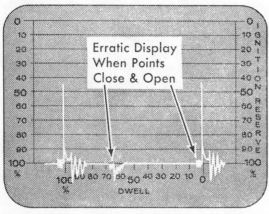

Defective contact points will cause erratic operation of the pattern when the points open and close.

and the other to the No. 1 spark plug wire. Both leads are shielded, and the shields must be connected to ground. To operate the equipment, turn the EXPAND control clockwise in order to turn on the scope. Start the engine and adjust its speed to 1000 rpm. Use an electric primary-actuated tachometer for this adjustment, and then remove the tachometer leads when the engine is ready for testing; otherwise, the tachometer will cause abnormal scope patterns.

DEVELOPING A NORMAL SECONDARY PATTERN. Turn all controls, except the EXPAND control, fully counterclockwise. Turn the PARADE control to spread the pattern to the desired width. Turn the HEIGHT control to raise the highest peak to the 50% line. Adjust the STABILITY control to show the correct number of cylinders and also to stabilize the pattern.

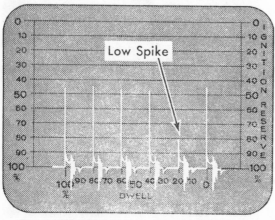

A low spike is an indication of a shorted plug.

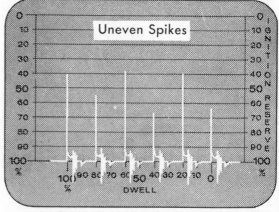

Two divisions in variation between spikes are allowed. If a greater variation exists, there is a defect in the high tension wiring or spark plugs.

Compressing the Pattern to Show One Cylinder in Detail. Adjust the EXPAND control to compress the pattern to the left side of the scope and adjust the HEIGHT control to register the peaks on the 50% line. Compare the height of each peak, and, if any varies over 1 division, it indicates a series gap between the distributor and the spark plug. This shows on the scope as a higher peak and can be caused by a high tension wire not making contact in the distributor cap, an open plug wire, or a wide spark plug gap.

Testing the Ignition Reserve. Remove any spark plug wire (except No. 1) and adjust the HEIGHT control until that cylinder peak reaches the top line. Observe the peaks of the other cylinders to determine the amount of ignition "reserve" left in the system. The normal reserve reading should be 60% or more. If there is not enough reserve, the following causes should be checked: wide spark plug gaps, burned distributor rotor, burned distributor cap points, center coil wire not seated fully in the distributor cap, condenser leaking, defective ignition coil, or high resistance between the breaker points.

Testing the Point Dwell. Use the EXPAND and PARADE controls to center the pattern of one cylinder on the bottom line. Normal dwell should be between 60% and 70%. Dwell time, when expressed in per cent, is the same for all engines regardless of the number of cylinders.

TROUBLESHOOTING THE IGNITION SYSTEM WITH SEPARATE METERS

In the absence of a scope, a battery of separate units must be connected to test the various components and circuits of the ignition system. To make a complete series of electrical ignition tests, it is necessary to have a coil-condenser tester, a dwell angle-tachometer meter, a timing light, and a volt-ohm-ammeter (the latter is also needed to test the charging circuit). Many manufacturers make various combinations of these meters and some add an air-fuel analyzer and mount the meters in an attractive panel in order to furnish a complete engine tune-up laboratory.

TESTING FOR PRIMARY CIRCUIT RESISTANCE

Generally, the primary circuit gives the most trouble; and most primary trouble can be traced to resistance between the contact points. A defective set of contact points usually has a black, oxidized coating over the point faces. Such contact points should be replaced. When testing for such a condition, a voltmeter is used to measure the voltage drop across the point set when current is flowing. A voltage drop of over 0.2 volt is considered sufficient reason for replacement. Two causes of contact-point oxidation are oil on the point faces and high voltage.

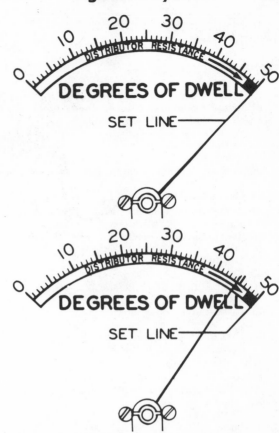

A dwell meter always contains a black section of the dial to read contact point resistance (black box at the right side of dial). After the needle is adjusted to the SET line (top), the button is released and the needle will register the resistance of the points. If the needle does not remain in the black box, the resistance is excessive and the points should be replaced.

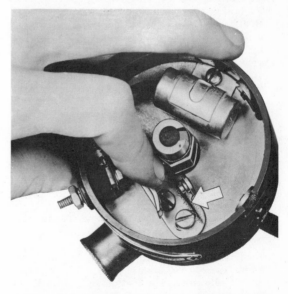

Oil on the contact point faces is a frequent offender of burned points. Its presence can often be detected by the smudge line under the contact points.

PRIMARY CIRCUIT VOLTAGE TROUBLESHOOTING CHART

VOLTMETER READINGS & TROUBLES

1. **V-1 should read not over 1 volt maximum while the engine is being cranked; otherwise check the following listed troubles:**
   1a. Open circuit from the battery side of the coil to the solenoid switch
   1b. Solenoid switch not closing the ignition circuit
   1c. Ground in circuit from coil terminal to the solenoid switch
   1d. Ground in coil

2. **With the ignition switch turned on, and the points open, V-2 should read normal battery voltage; otherwise, check the following listed troubles:**
   2a. Low battery
   2b. Points not open
   2c. Ground in circuit from the coil to the distributor
   2d. Ground in the distributor
   2e. Ground in the coil
   2f. Ground in the circuit from the coil to the solenoid switch or to the resistor

3. **With the ignition switch turned on, and the points closed, V-2 should read between 5 and 7 volts. If it reads over 7 volts, check the following listed troubles:**
   3a. Contacts not closed
   3b. Loose connection in the distributor
   3c. Distributor not properly grounded to the engine block
   3d. Defective contact points
   3e. Loose connection between the coil and the distributor
   3f. Resistor defective or incorrectly wired
   3g. Solenoid contacts remain closed
   3h. Coil primary open circuited

4. **If V-2 reads under 5 volts with the points closed and the switch turned on, check the following listed troubles:**
   4a. Loose connection between the battery and the resistor
   4b. Loose connection between the resistor and the coil
   4c. Defective resistor—open circuited or too high a resistance

5. **With the ignition switch turned on, and the points closed, V-3 should read 0.2 volt maximum; otherwise, check the following listed troubles:**
   5a. Contacts not closed
   5b. Loose connection in the distributor
   5c. Distributor not properly grounded to the engine block
   5d. Faulty contacts

6. **With the ignition switch turned on, and the points closed, V-4 should read 0.7 volt maximum; otherwise, check the following listed trouble:**
   6a. Loose connection from the resistor through the ignition switch circuit to the battery

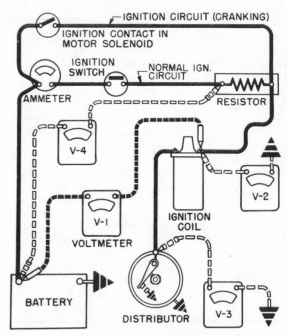

Primary circuit voltage troubleshooting chart. The various test positions of the meters are discussed in the text.

TESTING A CONDENSER

Three tests are generally made on a condenser, these are for: leakage, capacity, and series resistance. All condenser testers make these tests in similar fashion and have similar controls. They are: a circuit selector, a "set" knob, and a specification knob. The selector control connects the proper electrical test circuit in the instrument, as desired by the operator. The "set" control allows adjustment of the meter needle to a "set" line, and the specification control allows settings of the equipment so that a coil being tested can be compared with known standards.

Turn on the switch, allow an adequate warm-up time, and adjust the needle position to the "set" line. Now turn the selector knob to the CAPACITY position. Connect the leads of the tester to the condenser, which must be disconnected from its circuit. The meter will read the capacity of the condenser, which should be between 0.2 and 0.3 microfarad.

Turn the selector knob to the LEAKAGE position and read the leakage scale. The scales are color-coded to read GOOD or BAD. Now, make the series resistance test. Discard any condenser which registers in the BAD section of any scale.

TESTING AN IGNITION COIL

An ignition coil must be checked for open circuits and grounds within the case. An efficiency test is given to the coil so that its performance can be checked against known standards. These specifications are generally given by the manufacturer of the test equipment, as the standards apply only to his equipment.

After turning on the switch and allowing a proper warm up period, adjust the needle to the "set" line. Now turn the selector knob to the three positions shown on the instrument, making each test in turn. The scales are color-coded and labeled to read GOOD or BAD.

TESTING THE IGNITION SYSTEM FOR CONDITIONS CAUSING POWER LOSSES

Two common ignition system troubles, with regard to power losses, are late ignition timing and misfiring cylinders.

Late ignition timing causes overheating and loss of power. It can be detected by too smooth an idle, a deep-sounding exhaust, a low vacuum gauge reading, and a lack of "ping" on acceleration. Misfiring cylinders are characterized by a rough idle, a stuttering exhaust on acceleration, and a jerky vacuum gauge needle.

CHECKING THE IGNITION TIMING

A stroboscope should be used to check the ignition timing. The two leads of the test instrument are connected to the No. 1 spark plug wire and to a good engine ground. Some timing lights are equipped with a transformer to intensify the amount of light, and these have two extra leads, which must be connected across the car battery.

In use, the engine is idled as slowly as possible. Most manufacturers recommend that the vacuum line to the distributor be disconnected to make sure that no vacuum is applied to the vacuum advance diaphragm, which would cause an error in setting

A strobe light is used to set the ignition timing.

TIMING MARKS

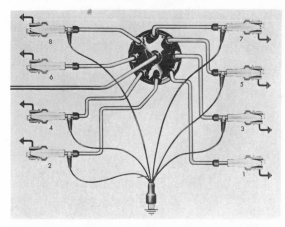

A set of shorting wires can be used to short out all cylinders except one. With the engine running on one cylinder, the relative efficiency of each cylinder can be compared. This test is more effective if a vacuum gauge is used to compare cylinders.

the distributor. Tape up the disconnected vacuum line to keep air from entering the intake manifold, which would cause the engine to speed up. Point the test light at the impulse neutralizer where an arrow is visible. The light makes the rotating flywheel appear to stand still. The arrow should appear directly over the spark-timing line stamped on the small flywheel. Some manufacturers stamp a series of degree marks on this flywheel so that the specification can be varied according to the type of transmission supplied. If the timing is not correctly set, the distributor should be rotated until the pointer appears to be directly over the specified mark. *CAUTION: This adjustment is the last one to be made in ignition work, because any change of the ignition contact point setting will change the timing.*

TESTING FOR A MISS

An engine is composed of several cylinders arranged to fire successively in order to develop a smooth flow of power. If one of these cylinders does not fire, it causes the engine to jerk, lose power, and waste fuel. A misfiring cylinder can be caused by a lack of spark, fuel, or compression.

The best test for a misfiring cylinder is to short out all the cylinders with the exception of one, and thereafter have the engine operate on each cylinder in turn. Any variation in power, or a cylinder which is not firing, will show up, because the engine will not run at all when the defective cylinder has to carry the load alone.

To make this test, loosen each high tension wire from its spark plug terminal before starting the engine, but do not disconnect any until needed. With the engine running fast enough to prevent stalling, short out each cylinder, except number 1, by removing its spark plug wire and laying it on the engine block. This is done so that the spark does not reach the spark plug and the cylinder cannot fire. To minimize the chances of getting an electrical shock when handling high tension wires, keep your fingers at least an inch from the metallic tip. *NOTE: Some mechanics use a set of shorting wires to connect all but one of the spark plugs to ground.* After all the cylinders, except one, have been shorted out, adjust the engine speed so that the engine runs as slowly as possible without stalling. Change the wires, one at a time. In this way, you can run the engine on each cylinder in turn. If a vacuum gauge is connected during this test, a very accurate comparative measurement can be made between the relative efficiency of each cylinder.

To FIND THE CAUSE OF THE MISS. Remove the defective cylinder spark plug wire; hold it 1/4" from the spark plug terminal, then start the engine. If a steady spark jumps to the spark plug terminal, the trouble must be fuel, compression, or a defective spark plug. If no spark jumps to the spark plug terminal, the trouble is in the ignition system.

To make a compression test, use a compression gauge or hold your thumb over the spark plug hole while cranking the engine.

If the engine misses on adjacent cylinders, the trouble may be a blown cylinder head gasket or a leaky intake manifold gasket. A blown cylinder head gasket will lack compression in either of the two affected cylinders. To test for a leaking intake manifold gasket, squirt water around the suspected surfaces. A sucking noise will indicate the entrance of the water into the manifold.

In some cases of adjacent-cylinder weak firing, a combination fuel pump may have a cracked diaphragm. The two cylinders receiving their fuel mixture from the intake manifold port, to which the combination pump is connected, will be weak because of air from the defective diaphragm entering the intake manifold and leaning out the air-fuel mixture. These two spark plugs are generally fouled with oil.

IGNITION SYSTEM TROUBLESHOOTING CHART

TROUBLES & CAUSES

1. **Primary circuit troubles causing misfiring or hard starting**
   1a. Defective contact points
   1b. Point dwell not set correctly
   1c. Defective condenser
   1d. Defective coil
   1e. Defective primary wire in distributor
   1f. Neutral-safety switch out of adjustment
   1g. Discharged battery
   1h. Low voltage due to resistance connections
   1i. Worn distributor shaft bushings
2. **Secondary circuit troubles causing misfiring or hard starting**
   2a. Defective spark plugs
   2b. Spark plug gaps set too wide
   2c. Defective high tension wiring
   2d. Cracked distributor cap
   2e. Defective rotor
   2f. Defective coil
   2g. Moisture on the ignition wires, cap, or spark plugs
3. **Ignition troubles causing poor acceleration**
   3a. Ignition timing incorrectly set
   3b. Centrifugal advance incorrectly set
   3c. Vacuum advance unit incorrectly adjusted
   3d. Defective vacuum advance diaphragm
   3e. Preignition due to wrong heat-range spark plugs, or to overheated engine
   3f. Spark plug gaps set too wide
   3g. Defective spark plugs
   3h. Cracked distributor cap
   3i. Weak coil
4. **Ignition troubles causing erratic engine operation**
   4a. Defective contact points
   4b. Sticking point pivot bushing
   4c. Worn distributor shaft bushings
   4d. Worn advance plate bearing
   4e. Defective ignition coil
   4f. Spark plug gaps set too wide
   4g. High resistance spark plugs
   4h. Defective high tension wiring

TROUBLESHOOTING A MAGNETIC-PULSE TYPE TRANSISTOR IGNITION SYSTEM

Faulty engine performance will be evidenced by one of the following three conditions: engine miss, surge, or the engine will not run. When troubleshooting, make the checks in the following order:

Engine Miss. The trouble can be due to carburetion, which should be checked out first. If the trouble is localized in the ignition system, first check the timing with a timing light. Then clean and adjust the spark plugs. Check the high tension wiring for brittle or cracked insulation, broken strands, and loose or corroded connections. The high tension leads in the coil and distributor cap should be pressed all the way down. Inspect the outside of the distributor cap and coil tower for carbonized paths, which would allow high tension leakage. Check the rotor and the inside of the cap for cracks and carbonized paths.

Check the pick-up coil continuity by separating the harness connector and measuring the resistance across the coil, which should be 300–400 ohms. Check the coil for ground by connecting an ohmmeter from either coil lead to the distributor housing. The reading should be infinite, otherwise the pick-up coil is grounded.

Use conventional ignition coil testing techniques; however, make sure that the tester is capable of testing this special coil. If the above tests are satisfactory, the engine miss is probably caused by a defective pulse amplifier. Replace the amplifier with a new one to check out this source of trouble.

Engine Surge. An engine surge, much more severe than that characterized by a lean carburetor mixture, will be evident if the two distributor leads

BREAKERLESS IGNITION SYSTEM TROUBLE DIAGNOSIS PROCEDURE

ENGINE SURGE OR ERRATIC MISS CONDITION

When the above condition exists, unless the following checks are performed first, it is likely that major components will be replaced unnecessarily, and the problem will not be remedied.

All the wiring should be visually inspected for brittle or cracked insulation, broken strands, and loose or corroded connections. The secondary leads in the coil and distributor cap should be checked to make sure they are pressed all the way down in their inserts. Rubber boots should be tight in place over connections. The outside of the distributor cap and the coil tower should be inspected for carbonized paths which would allow leakage of high voltage to ground. Also, remove the distributor cap so the rotor and inside of the cap can be checked for cracks and carbonized paths.

An engine surge condition much more severe than produced by lean carburetion may be due to the two distributor pickup coil leads being reversed in the connector body, or may be due to an intermittent open in the distributor pickup coil.

ENGINE HARD START OR WILL NOT RUN CONDITION

Disconnect any one spark plug lead and crank engine while holding end of lead approximately ¼″ from ground. CAUTION: Do not perform this test by disconnecting the coil to distributor secondary lead or damage to the amplifier may occur.

SPARK OCCURS

Reconnect spark plug lead. The problem is not in the primary circuits. Check fuel system, starting circuit, carburetion, also check secondary circuit as described under "Engine Surge or Erratic Miss."

NO SPARK OCCURS

1. Reconnect spark plug lead.
2. Connect a tachometer between coil positive (+) terminal and the black/pink wire at the 3-wire connector on left side of firewall.
3. Place selector on 1000 R.P.M. scale, then crank the engine and look for tachometer deflection.

NO DEFLECTION

Make the following tests to determine location of open, short, or abnormally high resistance in circuit.

DEFLECTION

Pinpoint the system trouble by performing "Ignition Distributor Check" detailed below.

CIRCUIT RESISTANCE TEST
(Using Voltmeter)

1. Connect voltmeter between the ignition coil positive (+) terminal and a good ground location.
2. Turn ignition switch to "ON" position and observe voltmeter reading.

0 VOLTS

Indicates an open in ignition circuit between the battery positive terminal and the coil positive terminal. If connections are good, insert a jumper lead between the black/pink and the black lead at amplifier connector.

READS 0 VOLTS — Indicates an open in the harness to amplifier unit. Repair or replace the harness.

READS 5-7 VOLTS — Indicates open in amplifier unit. Replace amplifier.

0-5 VOLTS

Indicates high starting by-pass resistance or high amplifier resistance. Move voltmeter lead from coil positive to black/pink wire at 3-terminal connector at firewall (use test prod).

METER READS OVER 7 VOLTS — Resistance in amplifier too high—replace amplifier.

READS LESS THAN 6 VOLTS — Resistance too high in starting by-pass wire. (Spec.: approx. .7 ohm)

5-7 VOLTS

This is the correct reading, however, when obtained at this stage of the check on a system that has not been functioning properly it would indicate improper triggering action of the distributor pickup coil or amplifier unit. Perform DISTRIBUTOR CHECK.

7-11 VOLTS

Indicates high resistance through coil and ground resistance wire. Move voltmeter lead from the coil positive to the coil negative (−) terminal.

METER DROPS TO 3 VOLTS — Ignition coil resistance high—replace.

DROPS TO 4 TO 8 VOLTS — Resistance wire has too high a value—replace. (Spec.: approx. .45 ohm)

BATTERY VOLTAGE (11-12 VOLTS)

Indicates open in primary circuit. Move voltmeter lead to negative coil terminal.

METER DROPS TO 0 VOLTS — Indicates an open primary circuit in ignition coil. Replace coil.

STAYS AT 11-12 VOLTS — Indicates open in ground resistor wire or connections. Repair or replace harness.

IGNITION DISTRIBUTOR CHECK

Check performance of the distributor pickup coil and the amplifier unit by employing either of the test methods described below.

OHMMETER METHOD

1. Detach distributor connector body from harness connector, and connect an ohmmeter to the distributor leads.
2. Slowly rotate magnetic pickup assembly through full advance travel and read ohmmeter. If reading is not within 500-700 ohms replace pickup assembly.
3. If the reading is within the 500-700 ohm range, disconnect one ohmmeter lead and connect to ground.
4. If reading is less than infinity, replace magnetic pickup assembly.
5. If reading is infinite, replace the installed amplifier unit.

DISTRIBUTOR SUBSTITUTION METHOD

1. Detach distributor connector body from harness connector and connect a spare distributor to the harness connector.
2. Connect a tachometer between coil positive terminal and the black/pink wire at the 3-wire connector on left side of firewall.
3. With the ignition switch "ON," turn distributor shaft by hand and observe tachometer.
4. If tachometer needle deflects, replace magnetic pickup assembly in distributor installed in engine.
5. If there is no needle deflection, replace the installed amplifier unit.

NOTE: Components of the ignition pulse amplifier unit are not serviced separately—only the complete amplifier unit is available for service replacement.

Roadmap for troubleshooting a transistorized ignition system.

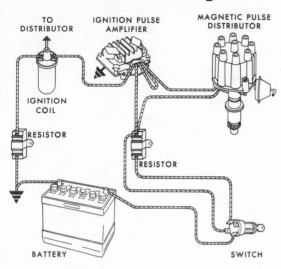

Circuit of a magnetic-pulse type transistorized ignition circuit.

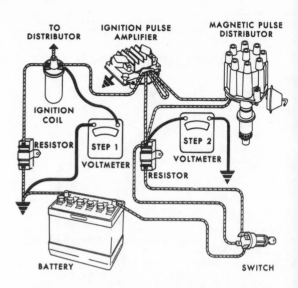

Primary circuit voltage troubleshooting chart for the magnetic-pulse type transistorized ignition circuit. The various test positions of the meters are discussed in the text.

are reversed in the connector body; or it may be due to an intermittent open circuit in the distributor pick-up coil. The white and green leads should be positioned as shown in the accompanying drawing.

A severe surge may also occur if there is an intermittent in the primary circuit to the magnetic-pulse pick-up coil. This can be caused by movement of the point plate under influence of the vacuum retard unit. To check this out, disconnect the vacuum line, plug it, and then operate the engine to observe its action.

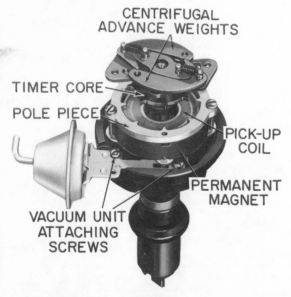

Magnetic-pulse type distributor with the cover off, showing the timer core and pole pieces. The ignition system fires when the pointed tips of the timer core just pass the pointed tips of the pole pieces.

Engine Does Not Run. If the engine does not run at all, remove a spark plug wire and hold it about ¼″ away from the block. If a spark occurs, the trouble is probably other than ignition. If no spark occurs, then check the ignition system as follows:

Check the high tension wires, distributor cap, rotor, and coil tower for defects. Check the ignition coil on a tester capable of testing the output of this special coil. In the absence of a coil tester, use an ohmmeter to check the primary for an open circuit or ground. Check the secondary for open and continuity. The secondary winding should have approximately 20,000 ohms.

Continuity Checks. Use a voltmeter to check the voltage at the two points shown in the accompanying circuit diagram. First, connect a voltmeter from the ignition coil positive terminal to ground (step 1). Turn on the ignition switch and observe the meter, which should be between 8–9 volts. If the reading is 12 volts, there is an open in the circuit between this point and ground. If the reading is zero, there is an open in the circuit between this point and the battery.

Now, connect the voltmeter from the other resistor to ground (step 2) and observe the reading with the switch turned ON. If the reading is zero, there is an open between this point and the battery. If the reading is 12 volts, there is an open in the circuit between the resistor and the ignition coil.

Check the pulse-generator pick-up coil for continuity and ground.

If the circuit checks out in the previous tests, and the engine still does not run, replace the pulse amplifier with a new one for checking purposes.

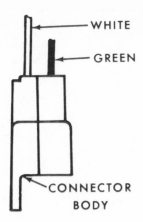

This is the correct position for the wires in the connector body. Reversing the wires causes a surging condition.

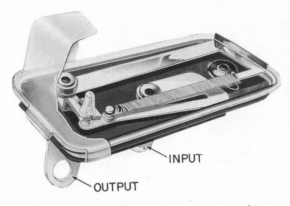

Cutaway view of the constant voltage regulator.

MAGNETIC-PULSE TYPE TRANSISTOR SYSTEM TROUBLESHOOTING CHART

TROUBLES & CAUSES

1. **Engine miss**
   1a. Ignition timing incorrectly set
   1b. Spark plug defects
   1c. High tension wiring defects
   1d. Carbon cracks in the rotor, distributor cap, or coil tower
   1e. Pick-up coil in the distributor open, shorted, or grounded
   1f. Amplifier defective
2. **Engine surge**
   2a. Leads to the distributor reversed
   2b. Intermittent circuit in the pick-up coil
3. **Engine does not run**
   3a. Defective high tension wiring
   3b. Cracked rotor, distributor cap, or coil tower
   3c. Open or shorted ignition coil
   3d. Open primary circuit
   3e. Open or shorted pick-up coil in pulse generator

TROUBLESHOOTING THE CONSTANT-VOLTAGE SYSTEM

Most automobiles contain a constant-voltage regulator which changes the varying voltage of the electrical system to a constant 5 volts in order to provide a stabilized voltage source for operation of the fuel and temperature gauges. The regulator consists of a bimetallic strip and a set of contact points which open and close due to the heating and cooling of the bimetallic strip.

To test the CV regulator, connect a low-reading voltmeter between the output terminal and ground. It is impossible to obtain a steady reading due to the vibration of the points; however, a fluctuating voltage reading between 0 and 7 volts indicates that the regulator is functioning satisfactorily. Because of the delicate nature of the unit, no adjustment is possible; if defective, it should be replaced.

To avoid the possibility of shorting the unit when testing, disconnect the battery ground cable before doing any work around the regulator.

CONSTANT-VOLTAGE SYSTEM TROUBLE-SHOOTING CHART

TROUBLES & CAUSES

1. **Temperature and fuel gauges read higher than conditions warrant**
   1a. Poor ground at CV regulator
2. **Both gauges read maximum when ignition switch is turned on**
   2a. Defective regulator
3. **Fuel and temperature gauges remain on E and C when the ignition switch is turned on**
   3a. Defective CV regulator
4. **Temperature indicator functions correctly but the fuel indicator shows higher or lower than actual fuel level**
   4a. Defective fuel indicator assembly
   4b. Defective tank sender unit
5. **Fuel gauge functions correctly but the temperature gauge indicates higher or lower than actual engine temperature**
   5a. Defective temperature indicator
   5b. Defective temperature sending unit
6. **Erratic temperature gauge operation**
   6a. Loose connections
7. **Erratic fuel gauge operation**
   7a. Loose connections
   7b. Defective tank sending unit

TROUBLESHOOTING THE CLUTCH

To test a clutch for slipping, set the hand brake tightly, open the throttle until the engine is running at about 30 mph road speed, depress the clutch pedal, and shift into high gear. Now, release the clutch; the engine should stall if the clutch is good. If the clutch is slipping, the engine will continue to run.

Check to see that the slipping is not due to a tight adjustment of the clutch pedal linkage. There must be 1¼" free pedal play before the clutch thrust bearing contacts the clutch pressure plate levers.

The only other clutch trouble is chattering when starting in first or reverse gear. Loose engine mounts and uneven clutch finger adjustments contribute to this trouble.

CLUTCH TROUBLESHOOTING CHART
TROUBLES & CAUSES
1. **Slipping**
   1a. Worn facings
   1b. Weak pressure plate springs
   1c. Pedal linkage out of adjustment
   1d. Sticking release levers
   1e. Pressure plate binding against the drive lugs
2. **Dragging**
   2a. Pedal linkage adjustment too loose
   2b. Warped clutch disc
   2c. Splined hub sticking on clutch shaft
   2d. Torn disc facings
   2e. Release fingers adjusted unevenly
   2f. Sticking pilot bearing
   2g. Sticking release sleeve
   2h. Warped pressure plate
   2i. Misalignment of clutch housing
3. **Noise**
   3a. Clutch release bearing requires lubrication
   3b. Pilot bearing requires lubrication
   3c. Loose hub in clutch disc
   3d. Worn release bearing
   3e. Worn driving pins in pressure plate
   3f. Uneven release lever adjustment
   3g. Release levers require lubrication
4. **Chattering**
   4a. Oil or grease on clutch disc facings
   4b. Glazed linings
   4c. Warped clutch disc
   4d. Warped pressure plate
   4e. Sticking release levers
   4f. Unequal adjustment of release levers
   4g. Uneven pressure plate spring tension
   4h. Loose engine mounts
   4i. Loose splines on clutch hub
   4j. Loose universal joints or torque mountings
   4k. Misalignment of clutch housing

TROUBLESHOOTING A SYNCHROMESH TRANSMISSION

Transmission noises can be heard much better with the engine shut off and the car coasting. By moving the shift lever from neutral into the various gearing positions, different gears can be meshed for testing purposes.

TRANSMISSION TROUBLESHOOTING CHART

TROUBLES & CAUSES

1. **Noisy with car in motion, any gear**
   1a. Insufficient lubrication
   1b. Worn clutch gear
   1c. Worn clutch gear bearing
   1d. Worn countergear
   1e. Worn countershaft bearings
   1f. Worn mainshaft rear bearing
   1g. Worn mainshaft front bearing
   1h. Worn sliding gears
   1i. Excessive mainshaft end play
   1j. Speedometer gears worn
   1k. Misalignment between transmission and clutch housing
2. **Noisy in neutral**
   2a. Insufficient lubrication
   2b. Worn clutch gear
   2c. Worn clutch gear bearing
   2d. Worn countergear drive gear
   2e. Worn countershaft bearings
3. **Slips out of high gear**
   3a. Misalignment between transmission and clutch housings
   3b. Worn shift detent parts
   3c. Worn clutch shaft bearing
   3d. Worn teeth on dog clutch
   3e. Improper adjustment of shift linkage
4. **Slips out of second gear**
   4a. Misalignment between transmission and clutch housings
   4b. Weak shift lever interlock detent springs
   4c. Worn mainshaft bearings
   4d. Worn clutch shaft bearing
   4e. Worn countergear thrust washers allowing too much end play
   4f. Improper adjustment of shift linkage
5. **Slips out of first/reverse gear**
   5a. Worn detent parts
   5b. Improper adjustment of shift linkage
   5c. Worn mainshaft bearings
   5d. Worn clutch shaft bearing
   5e. Excessive mainshaft end play
   5f. Worn countergear
   5g. Worn countergear bearings
   5h. Worn first/reverse sliding gear
6. **Difficult to shift**
   6a. Clutch not releasing
   6b. Improper adjustment of shift linkage
7. **Clashing when shifting**
   7a. Worn synchronizing cones
   7b. Excessive mainshaft end play
8. **Backlash**
   8a. Excessive mainshaft end play
   8b. Excessive countergear end play
   8c. Broken mainshaft bearing retainer
   8d. Worn mainshaft bearing

TROUBLESHOOTING AN OVERDRIVE UNIT

Overdrive troubles are usually due to improper operation of the electrical control system. Occasionally, it saves time to determine whether the trouble is electrical or mechanical in nature. For example, if the relay and solenoid click as road speed comes up through about 28 mph, and click again as the speed drops through about 22 mph, but the overdrive does not engage, the trouble is probably mechanical.

Mechanical Checks. With the overdrive control handle pushed in all the way, there should be 1/4" clearance between the shank of the handle and the support bracket on the dash. Raise the car and check the position of the overdrive control lever at the overdrive housing. The lever should be firmly against the stop at the rear. If the lever

To check the mechanical engagement of the pawl, ground the white wire and the solenoid stem should move in about ⅛".

isn't all the way back, the overdrive shift rail may be locking the pawl so that it cannot engage the balk ring gear.

With the engine off and the clutch engaged, shift the transmission into high or second, and shift the overdrive into the automatic position (rear). Now, the driveshaft should turn freely clockwise (from the front) but should lock up if turned counterclockwise. Leave the transmission in high or second, and shift the overdrive control lever to the locked-out position (forward). Now, the driveshaft should be locked against all rotation.

To check the mechanical engagement of the pawl with the balk ring gear, turn on the ignition switch and raise the car. Shift the overdrive lever forward to the locked-out position, and shift the transmission into neutral. Remove the cap from the overdrive solenoid. Turn the driveshaft clockwise (from the front) and, at the same time, ground the white wire with a jumper. This energizes the solenoid, and its stem should move in about ⅛". The solenoid plunger should move in about ½".

Keep the solenoid energized and shift the transmission into second or high gear to lock the output shaft against rotation. Shift the overdrive into the automatic position (rear). Again turn the driveshaft clockwise and observe the action of the solenoid stem. At no more than ¼ turn, the solenoid stem should move in approximately ⅜", which indicates the pawl has engaged the balk ring gear.

If the pawl engages the balk ring gear, the driveshaft will be locked against rotation in either direction. If the pawl does not engage properly, install a new solenoid and repeat the test. Now, if the pawl does not engage, the overdrive must be removed from the car for repair.

Electrical Tests. There are three electrical circuits in the overdrive control system: the governor, the solenoid, and the ignition interrupter circuits.

To Check the Governor Circuit. Turn the ignition switch on and off while listening for the relay and solenoid to click. If they click as soon as the ignition switch is turned on, either the governor circuit is grounded or the relay is defective.

To determine which condition exists, remove the kickdown switch wire from the TH SW (throttle switch) terminal on the relay and turn on the ignition switch. If the relay clicks, the relay is defective; if it doesn't click, the governor circuit is grounded.

To check the governor operation if the relay does not click when the ignition switch is turned on, disconnect the wire at the TH SW relay terminal. Raise the rear wheels off the floor. Connect a test lamp between the battery and the wire which was removed from the TH SW relay terminal. Start the engine and, with the transmission in high, increase engine speed until the speedometer reading goes through 28 mph. The test lamp should light at or about this speed. Slow the engine down through 22 mph. At or about this speed, the lamp should go out. If the test lamp lights and goes out at or about the indicated speeds, the governor and governor control circuits are working properly. If the lamp does not light at any time, replace the

Turn the driveshaft and the stem should move in about ⅜".

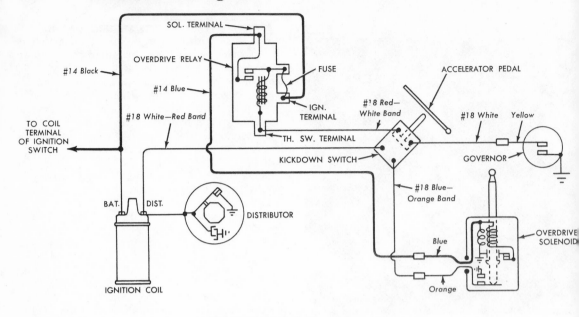

Wiring diagram of the overdrive unit.

wire at the TH SW relay terminal and continue testing as follows:

Turn on the ignition switch and raise the car. Disconnect the yellow governor wire from the white wire at the connector. Ground the white wire onto the transmission case. If the relay and solenoid click, the governor circuit is working properly from the TH SW relay terminal to the connector, and the trouble is in the yellow wire or the governor. If the relay and solenoid do not click when the white wire is grounded, the trouble is between the TH SW relay terminal and the connector.

To CHECK THE SOLENOID CIRCUIT. Stop the engine and turn on the ignition switch. Ground the TH SW relay terminal. If the relay and the solenoid click as the ground is made and broken, the solenoid circuit is working properly. If the relay does not click as the TH SW relay terminal is grounded, check the IGN relay terminal with a test lamp. With the ignition switch turned on, the test lamp should light when it is connected between the IGN relay terminal and ground. If it doesn't, the trouble is between the ignition switch and the IGN relay terminal. Next, connect the test lamp between the other end of the fuse and ground. If the lamp lit at the IGN end and not at the other, replace the fuse. With current at both ends of the fuse, connect the test lamp between the SOL (solenoid) relay terminal and ground. Ground the TH SW relay terminal. The lamp should light. If it doesn't, replace the relay.

With the relay working properly, the solenoid should click when the TH SW relay terminal is grounded. If it doesn't, connect a jumper from the SOL terminal to the short blue wire separated from

its connector near the solenoid. If the solenoid doesn't click when the relay closes with the jumper wire connected, replace the solenoid. If it does click, replace the wire from the SOL relay terminal to the connector.

To CHECK THE INTERRUPTER CIRCUIT. The overdrive unit cannot shift from overdrive to direct drive if the interrupter circuit does not ground the engine ignition momentarily when the driver depresses the accelerator to the floor. Inspect the white wire with the red band which runs from the ignition coil to the kickdown switch for proper installation. This wire must be connected to the DIST terminal on the ignition coil. Sometimes this wire is improperly connected to the BAT coil terminal during ignition work.

Raise the car and pull the blue wire with the orange band from its connector near the solenoid. Ground it to the transmission case with a jumper. Start the engine and run it at a fast idle. Reach under the accelerator pedal and push on the kickdown switch stem until it bottoms; the engine should stop. If the engine doesn't stop, the circuit is open between the DIST coil terminal and the connector.

To check the ignition grounding contacts inside the solenoid, disconnect the jumper and remove the solenoid from the overdrive unit. Attach the solenoid to the adapter so that the stem can extend fully when the solenoid is energized. Connect both solenoid wires at their connectors. Ground the governor wire with a jumper. Start the engine and run it at a fast idle. Reach under the accelerator pedal and press on the kickdown switch stem until it bottoms. The engine should stop; if it doesn't, replace the solenoid.

VERDRIVE TROUBLESHOOTING CHART

OUBLES & CAUSES

Unit does not engage
1a. Relay fuse blown
1b. Defective relay
1c. Defective solenoid
1d. Defective governor
1e. Defective rail switch
1f. Defective kickdown switch
1g. Dash control improperly adjusted
1h. Damaged gears in the unit

Unit does not release
2a. Defective relay
2b. Defective rail switch
2c. Sticking pawl
2d. Defective kickdown switch
2e. Defective gears in the unit

Kickdown mechanism does not operate
3a. Kickdown switch improperly adjusted
3b. Defective kickdown switch
3c. Defective solenoid

Engine stops when kickdown switch is actuated
4a. Defective kickdown switch
4b. Grounded solenoid

Car will not reverse
5a. Shift rail sticking

Harsh engagement
6a. Defective balk ring action

TROUBLESHOOTING A HYDRA-MATIC TRANSMISSION

PPLICATION: All General Motors products except hevrolet and Buick

Stall Test. Before any tests are made, the transmission fluid must be brought up to the correct level. Then a "stall" test should be made to determine engine and transmission performance. This test must be used with moderation because considerable strain is exerted on the drive line, differential gears, and axles.

To perform the stall test, warm the engine to operating temperature, connect an electric tachometer, set the hand brake lever tightly, and apply the foot brake firmly. Place the shift control lever in the DR position and depress the accelerator pedal to the floorboard. The engine will speed up until the friction created between the torus members equals the power output of the engine. Engine efficiency can be judged by the stall speed, which should be between 1800 and 1900 rpm. If the engine speed is less than 1800 rpm, the engine is in need of a tune-up. If the engine speeds up above 2000 rpm, then the neutral clutch, the front sprag, or the rear sprag is slipping. *CAUTION: Never hold the throttle open more than 1 minute, or damage will result.* If the engine speeds up to 2000 rpm, close the throttle immediately to avoid damage to the transmission.

Oil Pressure Test. Connect an oil pressure gauge to the take-off hole at the bottom of the rear pump. Start the engine and operate it for several minutes to warm the transmission oil to

normal operating temperature. (Approx. 175°.) Then check the pressure in all ranges, which should be 50 psi minimum in P, N, both DR ranges, and LO, with a maximum variation of 10 psi between ranges. The pressure may be higher in R.

Drive the car on the road and check the operating pressure in DR-right position at approximately 25 mph, which should be 90–100 psi. Now, move the selector back to the DR-left position so that the transmission will shift into fourth speed. The pressure should drop to 60–70 psi. Check the pressure in R by stopping the car and setting the hand brake firmly. Place the selector lever in R, apply the foot brake, and open the accelerator half way. The pressure should increase to 145–190 psi.

Road Testing. Additional troubles, such as noise, slippage, and improper upshifts and downshifts can be checked by driving the car over a test route which includes a hilly section to test for full-throttle upshift, slippage, and forced downshifts, a level section for testing upshift points, and a quiet section for testing for noise.

The upshifts should occur at the following speeds:

Shift	Left-Drive Range		Right-Drive Range		Lo Range	
	Minimum Throttle	Full Throttle	Minimum Throttle	Full Throttle	Minimum Throttle	Full Throttle
1–2	4–9	11–15	4–9	11–15	4–9	11–15
2–3	11–15	35–40	11–15	35–40	–	42–52
3–4	17–20	65–75	—	65–75	–	65–75

The downshifts should occur at the following speeds:

Shift	Left-Drive Range		Right-Drive Range		Lo Range	
	Closed Throttle	Full Throttle	Closed Throttle	Full Throttle	Closed Throttle	Full Throttle
4–3	15–11	70–28	70–60	70–28	70–60	70–28
3–2	10–6	25–14	10–6	25–14	45–39	45–39
2–1	8–3	12–3	8–3	12–3	8–3	12–3

HYDRA-MATIC TRANSMISSION TROUBLESHOOTING CHART

TROUBLES & CAUSES

1. **Slips in 1st and 3rd**
   1a. Front sprag clutch slipping
   1b. Front sprag clutch broken
2. **Slips in or misses 2nd and 4th**
   2a. Front unit torus cover seals leaking
   2b. Front unit torus cover exhaust valves sticking or missing
   2c. Front unit torus cover feed restriction or leak
   2d. Front unit torus cover signal restriction or leak
   2e. Low oil pressure
   2f. Coupling valve sticking
   2g. Sticking valves or dirt in valve body

Connecting a test gauge to make the oil pressure tests discussed in the text.

2h. Coupling snap ring improperly installed, or missing
2i. Limit valve defective
2j. Coupling passage restricted or leaking
2k. Front unit torus vanes damaged

3. Slips in all DR ranges
3a. Manual linkage incorrectly adjusted
3b. Neutral clutch slipping or burned
3c. Neutral clutch apply restricted or leaking
3d. Incorrect number of neutral clutch plates
3e. Low oil pressure
3f. Control valve defective
3g. Torus members defective
3h. Intake pipe "O" ring damaged or missing
3i. Pressure regulator valve stuck in pump
3j. Pump slide stuck

4. Slips in 1st and 2nd, DR range
4a. Rear sprag clutch slipping or improperly assembled
4b. Rear sprag clutch broken
4c. Neutral clutch burned, restricted, or the piston is sticking

5. Slips in 3rd and 4th
5a. Rear unit clutch slipping or burned
5b. Rear unit clutch apply restricted or leaking
5c. Incorrect number of clutch plates (rear)
5d. Accumulator defective
5e. Center support, leak at 2-3 passage
5f. Low oil pressure
5g. Accumulator valve stuck—3rd only

6. Slips in 3rd or in DR-right on coast
6a. Overrun clutch slipping or burned
6b. Overrun clutch apply restricted or leaking
6c. Sticking valves or dirt in valve body
6d. Overrun clutch passage restricted or leaking

7. Slips in 1st and 2nd in LO range on coast
7a. Low servo apply restricted or leaking
7b. Low band not anchored to case or broken
7c. Low servo piston and rod binding in case of servo and accumulator body
7d. Band facing worn or loose
7e. Anchor dowel pin loose or missing in case

8. No drive in DR range
8a. Manual linkage incorrectly adjusted
8b. Manual valve not engaged with drive pin
8c. Low oil pressure
8d. Pressure regulator stuck
8e. Front pump intake pipe improperly installed
8f. Front sprag broken
8g. Front and/or rear sprag incorrectly installed
8h. Rear sprag broken
8i. Front sprag inner race broken
8j. Rear sprag outer race broken
8k. Neutral clutch plates burned
8l. Neutral clutch piston stuck
8m. Control valve defective
8n. Front pump defective

9. No upshifts or erratic operation
9a. Governor valves stuck
9b. Broken governor rings
9c. Sticking valves or dirt in valve body
9d. G-2 bushing turned
9e. Front unit internal gear bushing seized to shaft

10. Misses 2nd
10a. Governor boost valve stuck closed
10b. Transition valve stuck away from plate
10c. Sticking valves or dirt in valve body
10d. Governor sticking

11. Misses 3rd or 2-4-3
11a. Transition valve sticking
11b. Sticking valves or dirt in valve body
11c. TV adjustment—too long
11d. Rear clutch
11e. Transition valve spring weak or broken

12. Locks up in 2nd and 4th
12a. Front sprag clutch broken
12b. Overrun clutch applied or sticking

13. Locks up in 3rd and 4th
13a. Rear sprag clutch broken
13b. LO band not releasing

14. Rough 2-3 shift
14a. Accumulator valve stuck
14b. Accumulator piston stuck

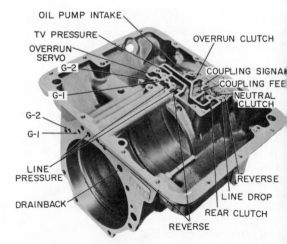

Passageway identification of the Hydra-Matic transmission. Air can be introduced through these passageways to check the operation of clutches and servos for testing or as assembly progresses.

14c. Accumulator gasket broken or leaking
14d. Restricted or leaking oil passages
14e. Broken accumulator spring
14f. Broken or leaking piston oil seal rings
14g. Control valve defective
14h. TV adjusted incorrectly
14i. Rear clutch pack slipping
14j. Case passages leaking or restricted

15. **Upshifts high**
15a. Throttle linkage adjusted too short
15b. Governor valves sticking
15c. Broken governor rings
15d. Sticking valves or dirt in valve body
15e. Leaking or restricted main line feed to governor

16. **Upshifts low**
16a. Throttle linkage adjusted too long
16b. Governor valves sticking
16c. Broken governor rings
16d. Sticking valves or dirt in valve body
16e. Leaking TV oil

17. **No reverse, slips or locks up**
17a. Manual linkage incorrectly adjusted
17b. Manual valve not engaged with drive pin
17c. Reverse piston apply restricted or leaking
17d. Low oil pressure
17e. Overrun clutch apply leaking
17f. Pressure regulator defective
17g. Neutral clutch not released
17h. Flash restricting neutral clutch exhaust port on manual body

18. **Selector lever will not go into reverse**
18a. Governor valves sticking
18b. Broken governor rings
18c. Reverse blocker piston stuck
18d. Manual linkage interference

19. **Reverse drive in neutral**
19a. Reverse stationary cone sticking

20. **Delayed 1–2 shift**
20a. Coupling valve sticking
20b. Governor boost valve sticking
20c. G-1 valve sticking
20d. Wrong spring on coupling valve

21. **Drives in LO range only**
21a. Rear sprag broken
21b. Neutral clutch not applying properly

22. **No forced downshifts, 4–3 or 3–2**
22a. Control valve defective
22b. Linkage improperly adjusted

23. **2–3 runaway or 2–1–3**
23a. 2–3 passage in center bearing support leaking
23b. Plug out of accumulator
23c. Rear clutch burned
23d. Valve body defective

24. **Will not go into P**
24a. Parking links broken
24b. Interference—parking mechanical
24c. Linkage improperly adjusted
24d. Parking pawl improperly adjusted

25. **Starts in 2nd speed**
25a. Valves sticking
25b. Governor sticking
25c. Governor boost valve stuck

26. **Drives forward in reverse and neutral**
26a. Neutral clutch piston stuck in applied position

27. **Lunges forward before backing up when placing selector in reverse**
27a. G-2 plunger stuck in the outward position
27b. Restricted neutral clutch release oil passage

28. **Noise occurs in P, N, R, DR, 1st, and 3rd**
28a. Front unit planetary gears defective

29. **Noise in P, N, R, DR, 1st, and 2nd**
29a. Rear unit planetary gears defective

30. **Noise in all ranges, especially during warm-up**
30a. Front pump worn
30b. Cut "O" ring on intake pipe
30c. Cut "O" ring on cooler adaptor sleeves

31. **Noise in 1–2, and 3–4, with hot oil**
31a. Front unit coupling leaks

32. **Noise in all ranges—loaded only in reverse**
32a. Reverse planetary gears worn

33. **Noise, clicking (low speed forward)**
33a. Pressure regulator defective
33b. Low oil pressure or level
33c. Coupling valve defective
33d. Governor defective

34. **Noise, buzzing**
34a. Pressure regulator defective
34b. TV valve vibrating
34c. Rear bearing defective if noise comes in at about 35 mph

35. **Noise, rattle or buzz under light load in 3rd and 4th**
35a. Torus cover—dampener spring loose

36. **Noise, squeak when engaging reverse**
36a. Low oil pressure or leak in front clutch overrun piston, or rear pump
36b. Clutch overrun piston, rear pump defective

37. **Noise, vibration**
37a. Flywheel out of balance
37b. Torus cover out of balance
37c. Front unit assembly out of balance
37d. Rear brake drum out of balance

TROUBLESHOOTING A ROTO HYDRA-MATIC TRANSMISSION

APPLICATION: Pontiac and Oldsmobile since 1961

Preliminary Tests. Always check the oil level before road testing. Erratic shifting or other malfunctions can often be traced to improper oil level. To check the oil level, park the car in a level position and set the selector lever in the P position. Let the engine idle until operating temperature is reached. Check the oil level indicator. If the level is low, add Automatic Transmission Fluid, Type "A," Suffix "A" until the level reaches the FULL mark.

The importance of proper linkage adjustment cannot be overemphasized. Improper linkage adjustment can cause rough erratic shifting, missing shifts, or the inability to select one or more of the ranges.

Make certain that the engine is operating at peak performance. The engine and transmission are designed to operate as an integral power unit. Failure of the engine to deliver peak power can result in improper shift characteristics and apparent transmission malfunctions. *CAUTION: Do not stall-test the transmission under any conditions.*

ROTO HYDRA-MATIC SPEED SHIFT POINTS

UPSHIFTS

Shift	Left-Drive Range		Right-Drive Range		Lo Range	
	Minimum Throttle	Full Throttle	Minimum Throttle	Full Throttle	Minimum Throttle	Full Throttle
2–3	14–18	33–40	14–18	33–40	No Shift Possible	
3–4	18–23	76–89	—	76–89	—	76–89

DOWNSHIFTS

Shift	Left-Drive Range		Right-Drive Range		Lo Range	
	Closed Throttle	Full Throttle Forced	Closed Throttle	Full Throttle Forced	Closed Throttle	Full Throttle Forced
4–3	20–15	84–68	84–72	84–72	84–72	84–72
3–2	16–13	29–25	16–13	29–25	52–46	52–46

To road check the unit, connect an oil pressure gauge to the upper of the two test holes on the left-hand side of the rear bearing retainer, and the pressure should check out as follows:

DRIVE RIGHT	MINIMUM	MAXIMUM
Steady at 25 mph	98.6	111.4

OIL PRESSURE TROUBLESHOOTING CHART

1. **Low oil pressure**
   1a. Oil level too low
   1b. Wrong boost plug or stuck
   1c. Pressure regulator valve malfunction
   1d. Strainer and "O" ring defects
   1e. Manual valve misaligned with quadrant
   1f. Foaming or cavitation of improper fluid
   1g. Internal leak
   1h. Stuck valve in control valve assembly
   1i. Front pump slide stuck in the low output side
2. **High oil pressure**
   2a. Pressure regulator valve stuck
   2b. Wrong boost plug or stuck
   2c. Manual valve misaligned with quadrant
   2d. Stuck valve in control valve assembly
   2e. Front pump slide stuck in the high output side

ROTO HYDRA-MATIC TRANSMISSION TROUBLESHOOTING CHART

TROUBLES & CAUSES

1. **No drive in drive range**
   1a. Neutral clutch slipping
   1b. Coupling defective
   1c. Sprag assembly slipping
   1d. Low oil level
   1e. Low oil pressure

   1f. Restricted passage in valve body
   1g. Internal leak
   1h. Manual linkage out of adjustment
   1i. Control valve assembly defective
   1j. Reverse cone sticking
2. **Drive in neutral**
   2a. Neutral clutch
   2b. Manual linkage
3. **No reverse**
   3a. Manual linkage
   3b. Low pressure
   3c. Reverse cone clutch
   3d. Restricted passage
   3e. Neutral clutch
4. **Drive in "right drive" or low range only**
   4a. Sprag assembly
   4b. Neutral clutch
5. **Forward drive in reverse**
   5a. Manual linkage
   5b. Neutral clutch
6. **Reverse drive in neutral**
   6a. Reverse cone clutch
7. **Drive in 3rd and 4th only**
   7a. Control valve assembly
8. **Drive in 1st, 2nd, and 4th only (might be reported as 2–3 slip)**
   8a. Control valve assembly
   8b. Coupling
9. **Drive in 1st, 2nd, and 3rd only**
   9a. Governor (G-2)
   9b. Control valve assembly
10. **Slipping 2–3 shift (can be reported as 2–4 only)**
    10a. Front clutch
    10b. Control valve assembly
    10c. Accumulator
    10d. Compensator body assembly
    10e. Low oil pressure
    10f. TV linkage
    10g. 2–3 oil passages

- **Slipping 3–4**
  11a. Coupling
  11b. Control valve assembly
  11c. Front clutch
- **Slipping all ranges**
  12a. Low oil pressure
- **Rough 2–3 shift**
  13a. Accumulator
  13b. Compensator body assembly
  13c. Front clutch
  13d. Front clutch passage
  13e. Control valve assembly
  13f. TV linkage
  13g. Coupling
- **Erratic shifts**
  14a. Governor assembly
  14b. Control valve assembly
- **High or low upshifts**
  15a. TV linkage (short—high upshifts; long—low upshifts)
  15b. Control valve assembly
  15c. Governor
  15d. TV lever
  15e. Governor oil passage
  15f. TV pressure
  15g. Line pressure
- **No engine braking intermediate or low range**
  16a. Overrun band
  16b. Overrun servo
- **No part throttle or detent downshifts**
  17a. TV linkage
  17b. Control valve assembly
  17c. Accelerator travel
  17d. Governor
- **Selector lever will not go into reverse**
  18a. Manual linkage
  18b. Reverse blocker valve
  18c. Governor
- **Selector lever will not go into park**
  19a. Parking linkage
  19b. Manual linkage
- **Noise sources**
  20a. Oil pump: moan in all ranges, more pronounced with hot oil in 1st and 2nd gear at approximately 1000 rpm
  20b. Oil pump: whine during the 3–2 and/or 3–4 shift
  20c. Front unit gear set: 3rd and reverse gear noises at low rpm
  20d. Rear unit gear set: 1st, 2nd, 3rd, reverse, and neutral gear noises at high rpm, with the loudest noise during the 3–4 shift
  20e. Coupling fill: whine during the 3–4 shift, with hot oil at low rpm
  20f. Coupling: whine in all speeds, except 3rd
  20g. TV valves and governor: buzzing
  20h. Damper: rattle at light load in 4th gear

ROUBLESHOOTING THE CAST IRON ASE TORQUEFLITE TRANSMISSION

PLICATION: All Chrysler Products through 1961

The Chrysler Corporation recommends that you
not stall-test their automatic transmission;
herwise, damage to the unit may result. They

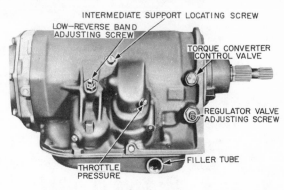

INTERMEDIATE SUPPORT LOCATING SCREW
LOW–REVERSE BAND ADJUSTING SCREW
TORQUE CONVERTER CONTROL VALVE
REGULATOR VALVE ADJUSTING SCREW
THROTTLE PRESSURE
FILLER TUBE

Oil pressure connecting points on the right side of the TorqueFlite automatic transmission.

recommend that hydraulic pressures be measured and a road test be given to pinpoint trouble.

Road Testing. First check the transmission fluid level and the condition of the engine idle. Good transmission operation depends on good engine operation. Make sure that the engine is operating at full efficiency; tune it, if needed. If the throttle linkage between the carburetor and the transmission has been disturbed, it will be necessary to readjust the linkage.

Before attempting to diagnose trouble, the transmission should be warmed up to operating temperature. A short drive of about 10 miles with frequent starts and stops will create normal operating temperatures in the engine and transmission.

1. First check for dragging by engaging the N (neutral) button and opening the throttle to an engine speed of 800 rpm.

2. Push in the R (reverse) button and note the shift time and smoothness of the shift. Back up the car and check for dragging.

3. Push in the D (drive) button and note the shift time and smoothness of engagement.

4. Accelerate the car with a very light throttle pressure. The transmission should upshift to second at approximately 10 mph and into direct drive at approximately 15 mph. Check the quality of the shifts.

5. Slow the car to approximately 15 mph. Then depress the accelerator pedal to a wide-open position (without going into kickdown). Check for slippage of the front and rear clutches. The transmission should not downshift at this time.

6. At a car speed of approximately 25 mph, depress the accelerator pedal fully to the floorboard; the transmission should shift to a breakaway gear. Check the quality of the shift.

7. Release the accelerator pedal and allow the transmission to upshift. Accelerate the car to 50 mph. Depress the accelerator pedal fully. The transmission should downshift to second gear; it should not downshift above 55 mph.

8. Release the accelerator pedal to a closed-throttle position. Check the quality of the "lift-foot" upshift.

TORQUEFLITE TROUBLESHOOTING CHART

ITEMS TO CHECK — See "Explanation of Index Items" — Perform Items: A, B, C, and G first	Harsh N to D or N to R	Delayed N to D	Runaway on Upshift and 3-2 K.D.	Harsh Upshift and 3-2 K.D.	No Upshift	No K.D. or Normal Downshift	Shifts Erratically	Slips in Forward Drive Positions	Slips in Reverse Only	Slips in All Positions	No Drive in Any Position	No Drive in Forward Ranges	No Drive in R (Reverse)	Drives in N (Neutral)	Drags or Locks	Grating, Scraping, Etc. Noises	Buzzing Noises	Trans. Hard to Fill—Oil Blows Out Fil. Tb.	Trans. Overheats	Impossible to Push Start	Starter Won't Energize
A. *Oil Level		●	●		●	●	●	●		●	●						●	●	●	●	
B. *Throttle Link Adj.			●	●	●	●	●														
C. *Gearshift Control Cable Adj.						●	●							●							●
D. Pressure Checks—Line, Lube, etc.	●	●	●	●	●	●	●	●	●	●	●	●	●						●		
E. K.D. Band Adj.			●	●	●	●						●			●				●		
F. Low-Reverse Band Adj.	●								●				●		●				●	●	
G. *Engine Idle	●						●														
H. Neutral Str. Sw.																					●
I. Handbrake Adj.															●	●			●		
J. Regulator—Valve Spring							●				●	●					●	●	●		
K. Converter Control Valve																	●	●	●		
L. Breather																		●			
M. Output Shaft Rear Bushing							●									●					
N. T.C. Cooling																			●		
O. K.D. Servo Band-Linkage			●	●	●	●						●				●					
P. L-R Servo Band-Linkage	●								●				●			●				●	
Q. Oil Strainer							●					●						●			
R. Valve Body—Bolts—Mating Surface		●	●	●	●	●	●	●	●	●	●	●		●						●	
S. Accumulator	●	●	●	●	●	●		●				●									
T. Air Pressure Check		●	●		●	●	●	●	●	●	●	●									
U. Governor				●	●	●								●			●				
V. Rear Pump																●				●	●
a. Front Pump—Drive Sleeve		●					●				●					●			●	●	
b. Regulator Valve Body, Gasket, Surface								●	●	●	●						●	●	●		
c. Front Clutch	●	●					●					●			●	●	●				
d. Rear Clutch	●		●	●	●		●					●	●		●	●			●		
e. Planetary Gear Set															●	●					
f. Overrunning Clutch						●	●					●			●						
g. Manual Valve Lever	●	●	●	●	●		●					●					●				

*Always Check Items A, B, C & G before performing any other operation.

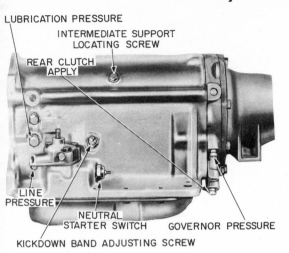

LUBRICATION PRESSURE
INTERMEDIATE SUPPORT LOCATING SCREW
REAR CLUTCH APPLY
LINE PRESSURE
NEUTRAL STARTER SWITCH
GOVERNOR PRESSURE
KICKDOWN BAND ADJUSTING SCREW

Pressure points on the left side of the TorqueFlite transmission.

9. Accelerate the car in kickdown gear with a wide-open throttle until the transmission upshifts. The shift should occur at approximately 65 mph. Check the quality of the shift.

10. Slow the car to 10–55 mph and engage the second-speed button. The transmission should downshift to second gear. Check for gear noise.

11. Slow the car to 15 mph and depress the accelerator pedal quickly to a wide-open position

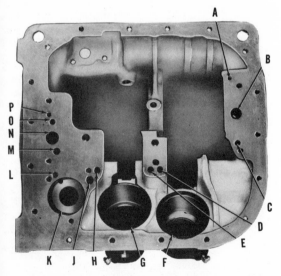

Identification of oil passageways in the TorqueFlite automatic transmission for introducing air to test the operation of the clutches and servos: (A) governor pressure, (B) rear pump inlet, (C) rear clutch apply (line pressure), (D) low-and-reverse servo apply (line pressure), (E) kickdown servo apply (throttle compensated), (F) low-and-reverse servo, (G) kickdown servo, (H) kickdown servo apply, (J) kickdown servo release, (K) accumulator, (L) front clutch and accumulator apply, (M) line pressure, (N) front pump inlet, (O) reverse upset (reverse block apply), and (P) line pressure gauge.

without going into kickdown. Check for kickdown band or front clutch slippage. The transmission should not downshift at this time.

12. Release the accelerator pedal and push in the L button. The transmission should downshift to second speed below 55 mph. The transmission should downshift to breakaway at approximately 25 mph.

13. Holding the accelerator pedal lightly, push in the D button at approximately 15 mph. The transmission will upshift to direct drive. Then coast to a stop; the transmission should downshift at approximately 10 mph. Check the quality of the downshift.

Checking the Hydraulic Control Pressures: LINE PRESSURE. Remove the pipe plug from the line pressure take-off hole located on the left side of the transmission case. Install a suitable pressure gauge. If the line pressure is not correct, it may be adjusted by loosening the locknut on the adjusting screw and turning the screw clockwise to increase the pressure or counterclockwise to decrease the line pressure. All line pressures should fall within the limits specified below. Any line pressure adjustment must be made with the transmission in D position, the engine operating at 800 rpm, and the rear wheels free to turn.

GOVERNOR PRESSURE CHART

Push Button Position	Rear Wheels	Engine (rpm)		Governor Pressure
		Std Governor	Hi Perf. Governor	
D	Free to turn	690–790	690–790	15 psi
D	Free to turn	1250–1510	1680–1860	45 psi
D	Free to turn	2560–2790	2850–3070	75 psi

LINE PRESSURE CHART

Push Button Position	Rear Wheels	Engine (rpm)	Line Pressure (psi)
R	Free to turn	1600	200–240
N	———	1200	85–95
D (Shifted into Direct)	Free to turn	1200	89–91
2	Free to turn	1200	85–95
1	Free to turn	1200	85–95
D	Free to turn	3500	93–100

NOTE: For cars equipped with "Ram Manifold" engines refer to charts below.

GOVERNOR PRESSURE CHART
(Ram Manifold Cars Only)

Push Button Position	Rear Wheels	Engine (rpm)	Governor Pressure (psi)
D	Free to turn	860–970	15
D	Free to turn	1830–2100	65
D	Free to turn	2550–2800	85

LINE PRESSURE CHART
(Ram Manifold Cars Only)

Push Button Position	Rear Wheels	Engine (rpm)	Line Pressure (psi)
R	Free to turn	1600	235–275
N	———	1200	100–110
D (Shifted into Direct)	Free to turn	1200	104–106
2	Free to turn	1200	100–110
1	Free to turn	1200	100–110
D	Free to turn	3500	108–115

REAR CLUTCH APPLY PRESSURE. Remove the pipe plug from the rear clutch apply pressure take-off hole located on the output shaft support. Install a suitable pressure gauge. The rear clutch circuit pressure should be checked simultaneously with the line pressure. The rear clutch apply pressure should not be more than 15 psi lower than the line pressure.

GOVERNOR PRESSURE. Remove the pipe plug from the governor pressure take-off hole located on the lower left side of the output shaft support. Install a suitable pressure gauge. All line pressures should fall within the limits specified.

LUBRICATION PRESSURE. Remove the pipe plug from the lubrication pressure take-off hole located on the left side of the transmission case. Install a suitable pressure gauge. With the shift control button in neutral and the engine idling at 800 rpm, the lubrication pressure should be 10–30 psi.

Testing with Air Pressure. The operation of the front clutch, rear clutch, low and reverse servo, and the kickdown servo may be checked by applying air pressure to their respective passages when the valve body is removed. To make the test, raise the car on a hoist, drain the transmission, and remove the accumulator cover and valve bodies assembly.

To test the operation of the front clutch, cover the accumulator piston bore to prevent the piston from being blown out. Protect yourself from oil spray by holding a clean cloth against the bottom of the case. Apply air pressure to the front clutch passage, located slightly toward the center of the transmission. A dull thud indicates that the front clutch is operating properly. Maintain the air pressure for a few seconds to check for oil leaks.

To test the operation of the rear clutch, apply air pressure to the rear clutch passage near the center rear end of the lower surface of the case. Listen for a dull thud which indicates that the rear clutch is operating satisfactorily. Check for oil leaks by maintaining the air pressure for a few seconds.

To test the kickdown assembly, apply air pressure to the kickdown line passage toward the center of the case in front of the kickdown servo. Observe its action when air pressure is applied.

To test the kickdown servo, apply air pressure to the compensated throttle passage toward the center of the case and to the rear of the kickdown servo. Observe the operation of the kickdown servo.

To test the low-reverse servo assembly, apply air pressure to the low-reverse servo passage, which is located toward the center of the case and in front of the low-reverse servo. Observe the operation of the low-reverse servo, lever, and band.

INTERPRETATIONS. If the clutches and servos operate properly, a no-drive condition or erratic upshift conditions indicate that the defects exist in the control valve body assembly, which must be removed for service.

TROUBLESHOOTING AN ALUMINUM CASE TORQUEFLITE TRANSMISSION

APPLICATION: Optional equipment on all 6-cylinder Chrysler products since 1960, V-8 since 1962

Line Pressure and Front Servo Release Pressure Checks. Warm the transmission to operating temperature, connect an engine tachometer, and raise the car on a hoist so that the rear wheels are free to turn. Connect pressure gauges to the pressure take-off points at the top of the accumulator and at the front servo release plugs. With the DRIVE button depressed, increase engine speed slightly until the transmission shifts into direct. Reduce engine speed slowly to 800 rpm and read the line pressure, which must be 52–60 psi. The front servo release pressure should be 45 psi or greater.

Disconnect the throttle linkage from the transmission throttle lever and hold the throttle lever at the detent position. Increase engine speed to 3500 rpm, and the line pressure should rise to 90–96 psi. The front servo release pressure should be 80 psi or greater. If the line pressure is not between 52–60 psi at 800 rpm, the valve body must be removed for service. If the front servo release pressures are less than specified, there is excessive leakage in the front clutch and/or front servo circuits.

Lubrication Pressures. Install a "T" fitting between the cooler return line fitting and the fitting hole in the case at the rear of the left side of the transmission. Connect a pressure gauge and check the pressure at 800 rpm with the throttle closed and the transmission in direct. The lubrication pressure should be 5–25 psi.

Rear Servo Apply Pressure. Connect a pressure gauge to the apply pressure take-off point at the rear servo. With the transmission control in REVERSE position and the engine speed at 1600 rpm, the reverse apply pressure should be 230–280 psi.

Governor Pressure. Connect a pressure gauge to the governor pressure take-off point, located at

ALUMINUM CASE TORQUEFLITE TROUBLESHOOTING CHART

Index	Item	Shift Abnormalities							Response								Miscellaneous					
		Harsh N to D or N to R	Delayed N to D	Runaway on Upshift and 3-2 K.D.	Harsh Upshift and 3-2 K.D.	No Upshift	No K.D. or Normal Downshift	Shifts Erratically	Slips in Forward Drive Positions	Slips in Reverse Only	Slips in All Positions	No Drive in Any Position	No Drive in Forward Ranges	No Drive in R (Reverse)	Drives in N (Neutral)	Drags or Locks	Grating, Scraping Noises	Buzzing Noises	Hard to Fill—Oil Blows Out Filler Tube	Trans. Overheats	Impossible to Push Start	Starter Won't Energize
A	Fluid Level		●	●		●	●	●	●			●	●					●	●	●	●	
B	Throttle Link Adj.			●	●	●	●	●														
C	Gearshift Control Cable Adj.						●	●							●							●
D	Engine Idle	●						●														
E	Pressure Checks Line, Lube, etc.	●	●	●	●	●	●	●	●	●	●	●	●	●	●							
F	Governor						●	●						●								
G	K. D. Band Adj.			●	●	●	●						●				●	●		●		
H	Low-Reverse Band Adj.	●								●				●			●	●		●	●	
I	Neutral Start. Sw.																					●
J	Breather																	●				
K	Cooling																			●		
L	Parking Brake Adj.																●	●		●		
M	Oil Strainer							●				●								●		
N	Valve Body Asb.	●	●	●	●	●	●	●	●	●	●	●	●	●	●		●				●	
O	Accumulator	●	●	●	●	●	●		●					●								
P	Air Pressure Checks		●	●		●	●		●	●	●	●	●	●								
Q	K. D. Servo-Band-Linkage			●	●	●	●						●				●	●				
R	L. R. Servo-Band-Linkage	●								●				●			●	●			●	
S	Rear Pump																			●	●	
a	Front Pump		●					●				●	●							●		
b	Front Clutch	●	●						●					●			●	●		●		
c	Rear Clutch	●		●	●	●			●				●	●			●	●		●		
d	Planetary Gear Sets																●	●				
e	Overrunning Clutch						●		●				●				●	●				
f	Converter										●										●	

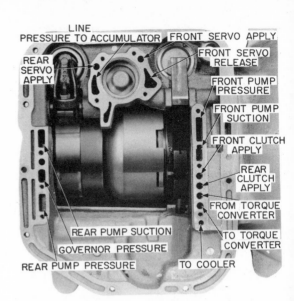

These are the points for testing pressure on the right side of the aluminum case TorqueFlite automatic transmission.

The oil passageways on the aluminum case Torque-Flite automatic transmission are useful for introducing air to test the clutches and servos.

the lower left rear corner of the extension mounting flange. The governor pressures should fall between limits given in the following chart:

GOVERNOR PRESSURE CHART

Engine Speed (rpm)	Pressure Limits (psi)
320	2–4
1000	28–32
1400	40–45
2800	73–83

If the governor pressures are incorrect, the governor valve and/or weights are sticking.

Throttle Pressure. No provision is made to check throttle pressure.

Air Pressure Checks. To check the front clutch, apply air pressure to the front clutch passage and listen for a dull thud which indicates

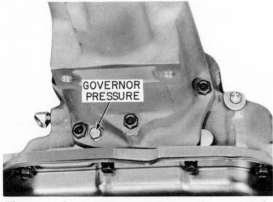

These are the pressure test points at the rear of the transmission.

that the front clutch is operating. Hold pressure on the system for a few seconds to check for excessive oil leaks.

To check the rear clutch, apply air pressure to the rear clutch passage and listen for a dull thud which indicates that the rear clutch is operating. Hold pressure on the system for a few seconds to check for excessive leaks.

To check the kickdown servo, apply air pressure to the kickdown apply passage. Operation of the servo is indicated by a tightening of the front band. Spring tension on the servo piston should release the band when the air pressure is reduced.

To check the low-and-reverse band, apply air pressure to the low-and-reverse servo apply passage. Operation of the servo is indicated by a tightening of the rear band. Spring tension on the servo piston should release the band when the air pressure is reduced.

Interpretations. If the clutches and servos operate properly, but no upshift occurs or erratic shift conditions exist, it indicates that a malfunction exists in the control valve body assembly.

TROUBLESHOOTING A POWERFLITE TRANSMISSION

APPLICATION: Optional equipment on all Chrysler products through 1961

Hydraulic Pressure Tests. To check the line pressure, install a pressure gauge at the line pressure take-off hole located on the front left side of the case.

To check the throttle pressure, install a gauge at the throttle pressure take-off hole located on the right side of the case. When checking throttle ressure, always follow by checking the throttle linkage adjustment.

Throttle Pressure Adjustment. With the throttle linkage properly adjusted, start the engine and push in the DRIVE button. *NOTE: When the manual control lever is moved into the drive range, engine speed will drop about 50 rpm.* The throttle pressure should read between 13–15 psi. To adjust, remove the throttle valve adjusting screw plug and catch the quart of transmission fluid that will drain. Insert an adjusting wrench and turn the screw out to increase the pressure. Replace the plug and torque it to 20–25 ft. lbs.

LINE PRESSURE CHART

Gearshift Position	Rear Wheels	Engine Speed	Line Pressure
R*	Free to turn	1400	225 to 275
N	. . . .	800	85 to 95
D*	Brakes applied	800	85 to 95

Engine must be at operating temperature.

THROTTLE PRESSURE CHART

Gearshift Position	Brakes	Throttle	Engine Speed	Throttle Pressure
D	Applied	Closed	Idle	13 to 15
D	Applied	Wide open*	1400 to 1500	80 to 90

*Do not hold throttle wide open for longer than a few seconds.

GOVERNOR PRESSURE CHART

Gearshift Position	Wheels	Car Speed	Governor Pressure
D	Free to turn	13 to 15	15
D	Free to turn	24 to 32	45
D	Free to turn	51 to 60	60

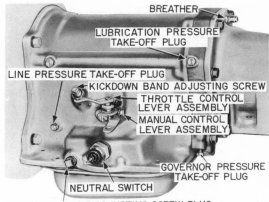

Oil pressure test points on the left side of the Power-Flite automatic transmission.

Move the accelerator pedal lever very slowly, to check the pressure rise. *CAUTION: Use the accelerator pedal lever located on the underside of the floor pan to speed up the engine, not the throttle rod.* With the throttle pressure correctly set and the linkage properly adjusted, throttle pressure will rise approximately 6–8 psi. Replace the fluid and tighten the plug to 10–12 ft. lbs. torque. Check the accelerator pedal height at wide-open throttle to see that there is sufficient clearance between the tip of the pedal and the floormat.

Governor Pressure Test. Install a pressure gauge at the governor pressure take-off hole, located on the lower left side of the output shaft support.

Direct Clutch Pressure Test. Install a pressure gauge into the hole in the kickdown servo. With the rear wheels free to turn, accelerate the engine slowly until an upshift occurs, at which time the pressure should show a rapid rise from zero to final line pressure (85–95 psi) in not more than 2 sec.

With an engine speed of not less than 650 rpm,

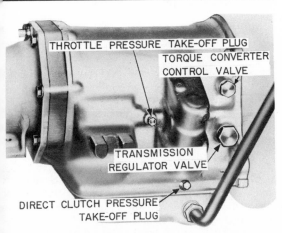

PowerFlite oil pressure test points on the right side of the transmission.

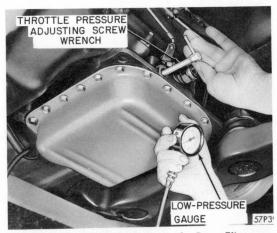

Adjusting the throttle pressure in the PowerFlite automatic transmission.

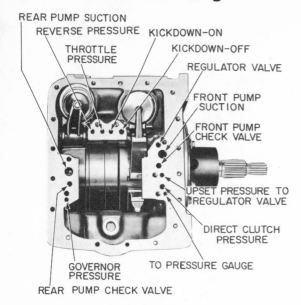

REAR PUMP SUCTION
REVERSE PRESSURE   KICKDOWN—ON
THROTTLE
PRESSURE   KICKDOWN—OFF
     REGULATOR VALVE
FRONT PUMP
SUCTION
FRONT PUMP
CHECK VALVE
UPSET PRESSURE TO
REGULATOR VALVE
DIRECT CLUTCH
PRESSURE
GOVERNOR   TO PRESSURE GAUGE
PRESSURE
REAR PUMP CHECK VALVE

Identification of oil passageways for introducing air to test the operation of the cluches and servos in the PowerFlite transmission.

with the transmission upshifted, the direct clutch pressure should read not lower than 10 psi below line pressure. Should a slow rise in clutch pressure take place, or if the clutch pressure is over 10 psi lower than line pressure, it is an indication of abnormal internal leakage.

Lubrication Pressure. Install a gauge into the oil cooler fitting from the lubrication pressure take-off hole, located on the left side of the case. With the engine running at 800 rpm and the transmission in neutral, the lubrication pressure should be 10 psi, minimum.

TROUBLESHOOTING A CRUISE-O-MATIC TRANSMISSION (AND FORDOMATIC BEFORE 1959)

APPLICATION: All Ford products, Rambler and Studebaker

Performance Tests: STALL-TEST. Before making a stall-test on the transmission, the fluid level should be checked and the engine tuned, if needed. The stall-test is made to determine if the bands and clutches are holding properly. *CAUTION: Do not hold the throttle open for more than 5 sec. at a time under these severe loads; otherwise, damage to the transmission is likely to result.*

INITIAL ENGAGEMENT CHECKS. Initial engagement checks are made to determine if band and clutch engagements are smooth. Run the engine until normal operating temperature is reached. With the engine at the correct idle speed, shift the selector lever from N to D-2, and from N to D-1. Observe the initial band and clutch engagements.

STALL-SPEED LIMITS

Selector Lever Position	Clutch Applied	Band Applied	Engine Speed (rpm)
D2	Front	Front	1350–1700
D1	Front	One-way clutch	1350–1700
L	Front	Rear	1350–1700
R	Rear	Rear	1350–1700

Repeat this operation in L and R. Band and clutch engagements should be smooth in all positions. Rough engagements are caused by high engine idle speed, high control pressure, faulty operation of the pressure regulator valve or of the main control valve.

SHIFT POINT CHECKS. Check the light throttle upshifts in D-1. The transmission should start in first gear and shift to second at about 12 mph, and then shift to third at about 22 mph. While the transmission is in third gear, depress the accelerator pedal through the detent. If the car speed is above 36 mph, the transmission should shift from third to second. If the car speed is below 24 mph, the transmission should shift from third to first.

Check the closed throttle downshift from third to first by coasting down from about 30 mph in third gear. The shift should occur at about 8 mph. In D-1, the car will freewheel if the driveshaft speed in first gear is higher than the engine crankshaft speed.

Partial-throttle downshifts in D-1 may be checked by using the service brakes as a load. With the transmission in third gear, and the car traveling about 30 mph, depress and hold the accelerator at half throttle. At the same time, apply the service brakes to the point where road speed is slowly reduced. The third-to-second, and then the second-to-first shifts should occur as speed decreases.

With the selector lever in the D-2 position, the transmission can operate only in second and third gears. Shift points for second-to-third and third-to-second are the same in both the D-2 and the D-1 positions.

If the transmission is in third gear and the road speed is above 28 mph, the transmission should shift to second gear when the selector lever is moved from D-2 to D-1 or to L. When the same manual shift is made below 20 mph, the transmission will shift from second or third to first.

Operational Checks. Operational checks are made to supplement the stall-test results. When the stall-test speeds are low and the engine is properly tuned, converter stator clutch problems are indicated. They can be checked by a road test. If the stall-test speeds are 300 to 400 rpm below the

SHIFT POINTS

Rear Axle Ratio	Automatic Shift Speeds (mph)								Manual Shift Speeds (mph)
	D1		D1 or D2		D1	D1 or D2	D1	D2	L
	1-2 Minimum Throttle	1-2 Maximum Throttle	2-3 Minimum Throttle	2-3 Maximum Throttle	3-1 Minimum Throttle	3-2 Maximum Throttle	2-1 Maximum Throttle	3-2 Minimum Throttle	2-1
2.69:1	10–14	43–54	14–25	69–81	7–10	63–76	28–36	7–10	20–28

values shown, and the car cruises properly but has very poor acceleration, the stator clutch is slipping. If the car drags at cruising speeds and the acceleration is poor, the stator clutch has been installed backward. When the stall-test shows normal speeds and the acceleration is good, but the car drags at cruising speed, the stator is seized.

Control Pressure Tests. Attach a pressure gauge at the transmission case rear face and a tachometer to the distributor in order to read engine speed. Set the parking brake and run the engine until normal operating temperature is reached. Compare your gauge readings with the specifications below:

CONTROL PRESSURE LIMITS

Engine Speed	Selector Lever Position	Gauge Reading (psi)
Idle........................	All	56–68
1000 rpm.................	D1 or D2	80–85
Stall (at detent)..........	D1 or D2	149–169
	R	196–216
Stall (through detent).....	L	196–216

Air Pressure Tests. To make the air pressure tests, drain the transmission fluid. Then remove the oil pan and the control valve assembly. The inoperative units can be located by introducing air pressure into the transmission case passages leading to the clutches, rear servo, governor, and into the front servo apply, release, and accumulator tubes.

FRONT CLUTCH. Apply air pressure to the transmission case front clutch passage. A dull thud should be heard when the clutch piston is applied. If no noise is heard, place your fingertips on the drum and again apply air pressure to the front clutch passage. Movement of the piston can be felt as the clutch is applied.

GOVERNOR. Remove the governor inspection cover from the extension housing. Apply air pressure to the front clutch passage. Listen for a sharp click and watch to see if the governor weight snaps inward, which indicates normal governor valve action.

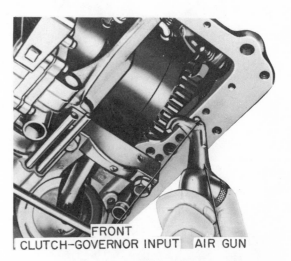

FRONT CLUTCH–GOVERNOR INPUT   AIR GUN

Applying air pressure to the front clutch.

A tachometer and oil pressure gauge can be connected and brought into the driver's compartment to test and adjust the control pressures.

GOVERNOR VALVE

Correct position of the governor for testing purposes.

REAR SERVO APPLY   AIR GUN

Applying air pressure to test the rear servo.

AIR GUN

REAR CLUTCH INPUT

Applying air pressure to test the rear clutch.

FRONT SERVO APPLY   AIR GUN

Applying air pressure to test the front servo.

REAR CLUTCH. Apply air pressure to the rear clutch passage. A dull thud indicates that the rear clutch piston has moved to the applied position. If no noise is heard, place your finger tips on the rear drum and again apply air pressure to detect movement of the piston.

FRONT SERVO. Hold the air nozzle in front of the servo apply tube. Operation of the front servo is indicated by a tightening of the front band around the drum. Continue to apply air pressure to the front servo apply tube, and introduce air pressure into the front servo release tube. Hold cloth over the release tube while applying the servo to catch the spray. The front servo should release the band against the apply pressure.

REAR SERVO. Apply air pressure to the rear servo apply passage. The rear band should tighten around the drum if the rear servo is operating properly. If either the front or rear servo is inoperative, remove the unit and apply air pressure directly to its passages. Proper operation of the servos indicates that the trouble is in the case passages. If the servo does not operate, remove and repair it.

If air pressure applied to either of the clutch passages fails to operate a clutch or operates both clutches at once, remove the output shaft. With air pressure, check the fluid passages at the output shaft aluminum sleeve for correct indexing with the shaft holes. Check the primary sun gear shaft assembly passages with air pressure to detect obstructions.

If the output shaft and primary sun gear shaft passages are clear, remove the clutch assemblies. Clean and inspect the malfunctioning clutch to locate the trouble.

CRUISE-O-MATIC TRANSMISSION
TROUBLESHOOTING CHART

TROUBLES & CAUSES

1. **Rough initial engagement**
   1a. Engine idling too fast
   1b. Throttle linkage out of adjustment
   1c. Rear band out of adjustment
   1d. Control pressures not up to specifications
   1e. Pressure regulator malfunction
   1f. Valve body needs cleaning

2. **1–2 or 2–3 shift points incorrect**
   2a. Fluid level too low
   2b. Throttle linkage out of adjustment
   2c. Manual linkage out of adjustment
   2d. Governor defective
   2e. Control pressures not up to specifications
   2f. Valve body needs cleaning
   2g. Inner and outer throttle levers out of adjustment

3. **Rough 2–3 shift**
   3a. Throttle linkage out of adjustment
   3b. Front band out of adjustment
   3c. Pressure regulator malfunction
   3d. Valve body needs cleaning
   3e. Front servo sticking
   3f. Rear clutch piston air bleed valve inoperative

4. **Engine overspeeds on 2–3 shift**
   4a. Throttle linkage out of adjustment
   4b. Front band out of adjustment
   4c. Valve body needs cleaning
   4d. Rear clutch piston air bleed valve inoperative

5. **No 1–2 or 2–3 shift**
   5a. Defective governor
   5b. Valve body needs cleaning
   5c. Rear clutch defective
   5d. Leakage in hydraulic system
   5e. Fluid distributor sleeve in output shaft defective

6. **No 3–1 shift**
   6a. Engine idle speed too fast
   6b. Throttle linkage out of adjustment
   6c. Valve body needs cleaning

7. **No forced downshifts**
   7a. Throttle linkage out of adjustment
   7b. Control pressures not up to specifications
   7c. Valve body needs cleaning
   7d. Inner and outer throttle levers out of adjustment

8. **Runaway engine on forced downshift**
   8a. Front band needs adjusting
   8b. Pressure regulator malfunction
   8c. Valve body needs cleaning
   8d. Front servo sticking
   8e. Leakage in hydraulic system

9. **Rough 3–2 or 3–1 shift at closed throttle**
   9a. Engine idle speed too fast
   9b. Throttle linkage out of adjustment
   9c. Valve body needs cleaning

10. **Creeps excessively in D-1 or D-2**
    10a. Engine idle speed too fast

11. **Slips or chatters in first gear**
    11a. Fluid level too low
    11b. Throttle linkage out of adjustment
    11c. Rear band out of adjustment
    11d. Control pressures not up to specifications
    11e. Pressure regulator malfunction
    11f. Valve body needs cleaning

11g. Inner and outer throttle levers out of adjustment
11h. Front clutch defective
11i. Leakage in hydraulic system
11j. Fluid distributor sleeve in output shaft defective
11k. Planetary one-way clutch slipping

12. **Slips or chatters in second gear**
    12a. Fluid level too low
    12b. Throttle linkage out of adjustment
    12c. Front band out of adjustment
    12d. Control pressures not up to specifications
    12e. Pressure regulator malfunction
    12f. Valve body needs cleaning
    12g. Front servo sticking
    12h. Front clutch defective
    12i. Leakage in hydraulic system

13. **Slips or chatters in reverse**
    13a. Fluid level too low
    13b. Throttle linkage out of adjustment
    13c. Rear band out of adjustment
    13d. Control pressures not up to specifications
    13e. Pressure regulator malfunction
    13f. Valve body needs cleaning
    13g. Rear servo sticking
    13h. Rear clutch defective
    13i. Leakage in hydraulic system
    13j. Fluid distributor sleeve in output shaft defective

14. **No drive in D-1**
    14a. Manual linkage out of adjustment
    14b. Valve body needs cleaning
    14c. Planetary one-way clutch slipping

15. **No drive in D-2**
    15a. Front band out of adjustment
    15b. Valve body needs cleaning
    15c. Front clutch defective
    15d. Leakage in hydraulic system
    15e. Fluid distributor sleeve in output shaft defective

16. **No drive in L**
    16a. Manual linkage out of adjustment
    16b. Rear band out of adjustment
    16c. Rear servo sticking
    16d. Valve body needs cleaning
    16e. Leakage in hydraulic system
    16f. Fluid distributor sleeve in output shaft defective

17. **No drive in R**
    17a. Rear band out of adjustment
    17b. Rear servo sticking
    17c. Valve body needs cleaning
    17d. Rear clutch defective
    17e. Leakage in hydraulic system
    17f. Fluid distributor sleeve in output shaft defective

18. **No drive in any selector lever position**
    18a. Fluid level too low
    18b. Manual linkage out of adjustment
    18c. Control pressures not up to specifications
    18d. Pressure regulator malfunction
    18e. Valve body needs cleaning
    18f. Leakage in hydraulic system

19. **Lockup in D-1**
    19a. Manual linkage out of adjustment
    19b. Rear servo sticking
    19c. Front servo sticking
    19d. Rear clutch defective

19e. Parking linkage out of adjustment
19f. Leakage in hydraulic system
20. **Lockup in D-2**
20a. Manual linkage out of adjustment
20b. Rear band out of adjustment
20c. Rear servo sticking
20d. Front servo sticking
20e. Rear clutch defective
20f. Parking linkage out of adjustment
20g. Leakage in hydraulic system
21. **Lockup in L**
21a. Front band out of adjustment
21b. Front servo sticking
21c. Valve body needs cleaning
21d. Rear clutch defective
21e. Parking linkage out of adjustment
21f. Leakage in hydraulic system
22. **Lockup in R**
22a. Front band out of adjustment
22b. Front servo sticking
22c. Front clutch defective
22d. Parking linkage out of adjustment
22e. Leakage in hydraulic system
23. **Parking lock binds or does not hold**
23a. Manual linkage out of adjustment
23b. Parking linkage out of adjustment
24. **Engine cannot be started by pushing car**
24a. Fluid level too low
24b. Manual linkage out of adjustment
24c. Pressure regulator malfunction
24d. Valve body needs cleaning
24e. Rear pump worn
24f. Leakage in hydraulic system
25. **Transmission overheats**
25a. Oil cooler defective
25b. Pressure regulator malfunction
25c. Converter one-way clutch slipping
26. **Poor acceleration**
26a. Converter one-way clutch slipping
27. **Transmission noisy in N**
27a. Pressure regulator malfunction
27b. Engine rear oil seal defective
27c. Front clutch defective
27d. Front pump defective
28. **Transmission noisy in any gear**
28a. Pressure regulator malfunction
28b. Planetary assembly worn
28c. Front clutch defective
28d. Rear clutch defective
28e. Front pump worn
29. **Transmission noisy in P**
29a. Pressure regulator malfunction
29b. Front pump worn
30. **Transmission noisy during coast at 30–20 mph in N with engine shut off**
30a. Rear pump worn

TROUBLESHOOTING A FORDOMATIC (ALUMINUM CASE) TRANSMISSION

APPLICATION: All Ford products, 1959-64

Preliminary Tests. Whenever transmission trouble is indicated, the following items must be checked in the order given below: (1) Check the fluid level. Also, note whether the fluid smells from burnt clutch plate material. (2) Check engine idle

speed and dashpot adjustments. (3) Check the manual linkage adjustment. (4) Check the throttle linkage adjustment.

Stall-Test. Before making a stall-test, check the engine coolant level and the transmission fluid level. Run the engine in neutral at about 1200 rpm until operating temperature is reached. Attach a tachometer to the engine so that it can be read in the driver's compartment. Apply the service and parking brakes firmly. Shift the selector lever to D, L, or R, and depress the accelerator to the floor. *CAUTION: Do not hold the throttle open for more than 5 sec. or damage to the transmission will result. CAUTION: If the tachometer readings exceed the high limit, or engine run-away is apparent, release the accelerator pedal immediately to prevent further damage.* Between tests, run the engine for at least 2 min. at 1200 rpm with the transmission in N to allow the converter fluid to cool. Compare the tachometer and pressure gauge readings with those specified in the accompanying tables.

STALL-SPEED LIMITS

Engine Model	Engine Speed (rpm)
223 Six	1370–1570
292 V-8	1590–1790
352 V-8 (Dual Carburetor)	1625–1825
352 V-8 (4-Barrel Carburetor)	1645–1845

Stall-Test Interpretations. Stall-tests require careful interpretation, because the engine, torque converter, and transmission are all under test at the same time. If the engine runs away in D or L, but is held within limits in R, the low band is slipping. If the stall-test is normal in R, it is probable that the engine, torque converter, and control pressure in the transmission are normal, and that the trouble is confined to the low servo and band. In this case, the band should be adjusted and the test repeated in D and L. If the band still slips, attach a pressure gauge and check the control pressure before dropping the pan to inspect the servo and band.

If the engine runs away in R, but is held within limits in D and L, the reverse band is slipping. Because of the time required to adjust the reverse band, the control pressure should be checked first.

The transmission clutch (high) cannot be stall-tested since it operates only at road speeds above 15 mph.

Should the converter stator clutch fail to operate properly, maximum engine speed will be about 1200 rpm. A second check should be made on the road if a defective converter is suspected. If the unit is defective, acceleration to 30 mph will be

FORDOMATIC DIAGNOSIS GUIDE

Trouble Symptoms	Items to Check	
	Transmission in Car	Transmission Out of Car
Harsh initial engagement in D, L and R	D B	
Slips or chatters in D or L	A B E H F K	a e
Slips or chatters in R	A B E I F K	b f n
Creeps excessively in D	D	
Engine overspeeds (buzz-up) during 1–2 shift	A L B E H F G	g j h
Momentary lockup during 1–2 shift	A B E H	a j k
Severe 2–1 shift during coast-down	D B G E	
No 1–2 shift in D	A L B C J Q	a d j p
Delayed 1–2 shift	B J	d m
Slips continuously after 1–2 shift	L A B E F	j g
No 2–1 forced downshift (kickdown)	B G	d
No 2–1 shift during coast-down	G J	
Fluid forced out vent	A M O P	
Transmission overheats	E R N	
Acceleration is normal—maximum speed about 50 mph		i
Acceleration very poor—operation above 30 mph at steady throttle normal		i
Engine does not start by pushing car	A C G	c d
Parking lock does not hold, or binds	C	l o

KEY TO DIAGNOSIS GUIDE

A	Fluid level	a	Low servo and band
B	Throttle linkage	b	Reverse servo and band
C	Manual linkage	c	Rear pump
D	Engine idle speed	d	Leakage in control pressure main circuit
E	Control pressure check	e	Leakage in low servo apply circuit
F	Air pressure check	f	Leakage in reverse servo apply circuit
G	Control valve body	g	Leakage in clutch apply or low servo release
H	Low band adjustment	h	Planetary gears
I	Reverse band adjustment	i	Converter one-way clutch
J	Governor	j	High clutch
K	Engine—transmission mounts	k	Low servo piston return spring
L	Fluid odor; check for burned clutch plates	l	Parking linkage
M	Transmission external vent	m	Low servo piston check valve
N	Cooler; flow check	n	Cracked or broken rear band anchor
O	Fluid; aeration check	o	Front band installed backward—strut out of position
P	Fluid; check for engine coolant contamination		
Q	High clutch piston		
R	Converter cooling air passages	p	High clutch piston

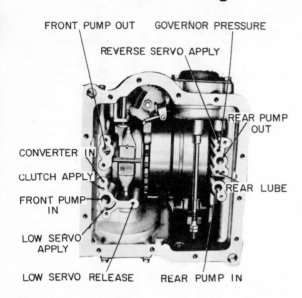

FRONT PUMP OUT   GOVERNOR PRESSURE

REVERSE SERVO APPLY

REAR PUMP OUT

CONVERTER IN

CLUTCH APPLY

FRONT PUMP IN

REAR LUBE

LOW SERVO APPLY

LOW SERVO RELEASE   REAR PUMP IN

Oil passageways that can be used to test the servo and clutch operation.

poor, but nearly normal above this speed. Should the stator clutch freeze up, the stall-test rpm will be normal, but maximum road speed will be about 50 mph.

Control Pressure Checks. When the preliminary checks have not indicated the cause of trouble, the control pressures should be checked before the transmission is removed.

Attach a gauge to the pressure line to show the pressure between the front pump and the front pump check valve. This pressure is regulated by the control pressure regulator valve and is the transmission control pressure. As long as the rear wheels are not turning, this pressure is supplied by the front pump only. When the car is driven with the gauge attached, the pressure will fall off suddenly from 70 psi to 5 psi at about 50 mph. This sudden pressure drop is normal and indicates that rear pump pressure has closed the front pump check valve to take over the complete fluid supply job. If this sudden pressure drop does not occur, either the rear pump or the front pump check valve is not operating properly. *CAUTION: In the interest of safety, the rear wheels must not be allowed to turn; otherwise, the transmission may shift and the car lurch off the hoist.*

In the D position, the control pressure should rise from 46–56 psi, at engine idle, to 77–84 psi at 1000 rpm. In the D, L, and R positions, the control pressure should rise to 170–192 psi at wide-open throttle (stall-test). If this pressure rise does not occur, there are four probable causes: throttle linkage, throttle and compensator pressure, pump capacity, and excessive leakage. Before the control valve body or transmission is removed for further inspection, the following checks should be made:

1. Check the pressure rise in D, L, and R. If the pressure rise is normal in any one position, throttle linkage, throttle and compensator pressures, and capacity are normal. The probable cause is leakage in the hydraulic system upstream from the manual valve.

2. To check the operation of the throttle linkage, disconnect the turnbuckle from the accelerator shaft and lever. Place the selector lever in the P position. Adjust engine speed to 1000 rpm, push down on the throttle control rod, and observe the pressure gauge, which should rise to the 170–192 psi range, which means that pump capacity, main system leakage, throttle and compensator pressures and throttle linkage are normal. The trouble probably is due to leakage in the low servo apply line.

3. If the pressure does not rise as the throttle control rod is pushed down, raise and lower the throttle control rod and feel for compression of the throttle valve spring as the rod moves downward. Check for loose throttle levers on the shaft by pushing the rod down firmly against the stop inside of the transmission.

Performance Tests. Performance tests should be made only after all preliminary checks have been made. The first check should be made on governor action. The accompanying table shows the various control pressures that should result with a wide-open throttle at various road speeds. The purpose is to indicate the rate at which the control pressure decreases when governor pressure is normal. If the gauge readings do not drop with increased road speed, the governor or the compensator valve may not be operating properly. If, however, the readings were normal with the car standing still at idle and stall, the compensator valve is almost certainly operating properly, and the fault must be with the governor.

Air Pressure Checks. Inoperative units can be located by substituting air pressure for fluid

FLUID PRESSURE LIMITS

Engine Speed	Selector Lever Position	Gauge Reading (psi)	
		144 cu. in. Six Engine	170 cu. in. Six and All V-8 Engines
Idle	All	40–48	46–56
1200 rpm	D	53–57	78–82
Stall	D, L and R	135–155	170–192

pressure to determine the location of a malfunction. With the selector lever at D or L, a no-drive condition may be caused by an inoperative reverse band. Failure to shift into high may be caused by excessive leakage in the clutch apply and low band release circuits.

TROUBLESHOOTING THE FORD C-4 AUTOMATIC DUAL RANGE TRANSMISSION

APPLICATION: Ford products since 1964

FLUID LEVEL

Check the transmission fluid level. A low fluid level can affect the operation of the transmission and may indicate fluid leaks that could cause transmission damage. A fluid level that is too high will cause the fluid to become aerated, which will cause low control pressures, and the aerated fluid may be forced out of the vent.

ENGINE IDLE SPEED

Check and, if necessary, adjust the engine idle speed. If the idle speed is too low, the engine will run roughly. An idle speed that is too high will cause the car to creep when the transmission is shifted into gear and will cause rough transmission engagement.

ANTI-STALL DASHPOT

After the engine idle speed has been properly adjusted, check the anti-stall dashpot clearance. Adjust if necessary.

MANUAL LINKAGE

Correct manual linkage adjustment is necessary to position the manual valve for proper fluid pressure direction to the different transmission components. Improperly adjusted manual linkage may cause cross-leakage and subsequent transmission failure.

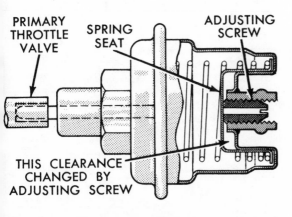

Vacuum diaphragm unit and adjusting screw discussed in the text.

CONTROL PRESSURE AND VACUUM DIAPHRAGM UNIT

When the vacuum diaphragm unit is operating properly and the downshift linkage is adjusted correctly, all the transmission shifts (automatic and kickdown) should occur within the specified road speed limits.

If the automatic shifts do not occur within limits or the transmission slips during shift points, the following procedure is suggested to separate engine, transmission, linkage, and diaphragm unit or valve body problems. (1) Attach a tachometer to the engine and a vacuum gauge to the transmission vacuum line at the vacuum unit. (2) Attach a pressure gauge to the control pressure outlet at the transmission. (3) Firmly apply the parking brake and start the engine. (4) Adjust the engine idle speed to the specified rpm. If the engine idle speed cannot be brought within limits by adjustment at the carburetor idle adjustment screw, check the throttle and downshift linkage for a binding condition. If the linkage is satisfactory, check for vacuum leaks in the transmission diaphragm unit and its connecting tubes and hoses. Check all other vacuum operated units (such as the power brake) for vacuum leaks.

VACUUM UNIT CHECK

To check the vacuum unit for diaphragm leakage, remove the unit from the transmission. Use a distributor tester equipped with a vacuum pump. Set the regulator knob so that the vacuum gauge reads 18″ Hg with the end of the vacuum hose blocked off.

Then connect the vacuum hose to the transmission vacuum unit. If the gauge still reads 18″ Hg, the vacuum unit diaphragm is not leaking. As the hose is removed from the transmission vacuum unit, hold your finger over the end of the control rod. When the hose is removed, the internal spring of the vacuum unit should push the control rod outward.

CONTROL PRESSURE CHECK—AT ENGINE IDLE

With the transmission in neutral, and the engine at the correct idle speed, the vacuum gauge should show a minimum of 18″ Hg. If the vacuum reading is lower than 18″ Hg, either an engine problem is indicated or there is a leakage in the vacuum line. Make necessary repairs to obtain a minimum vacuum reading of 18″ Hg.

At engine idle, depress and release the accelerator pedal quickly and observe the vacuum gauge. The amount of vacuum should decrease and increase with the changes in throttle openings. If the vacuum response to changes in throttle opening is too slow, the vacuum line to the diaphragm unit could be restricted. Make the necessary repairs before completing the test.

At engine idle, check the transmission control

CONTROL PRESSURE TAKE-OFF HOLE

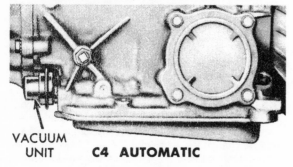

VACUUM
UNIT   **C4 AUTOMATIC**

Vacuum diaphragm unit and the control pressure connecting point.

pressure gauge at all selector lever positions. Transmission control pressures should agree with the specifications as outlined in the table.

CONTROL PRESSURE INCREASE CHECK

The control pressure increase should be checked in all ranges except Park and Neutral. Shift the transmission into D-1, D-2, L and R and check the control pressure increase in each range. With the correct control pressure at engine idle, advance the throttle until the engine vacuum reading falls between 17.5″–16.5″ Hg. As the vacuum gauge reading decreases to these specifications, the control pressure should start to increase.

Control pressure increase may be noted immediately when the throttle is opened due to the increased pump output, resulting from increased engine rpm. When this happens, the pressure increase point can be checked by using a distributor vacuum tester. Install the distributor tester vacuum line on the diaphragm assembly. Adjust the tester to provide over 18″ Hg of vacuum. Increase the engine speed to 600-700 rpm. Reduce the tester vacuum reading through the 17.5″–16.5″ Hg range and observe the transmission pressure gauge for the pressure increase.

CONTROL PRESSURE CHECK AT 10 INCHES OF VACUUM

A control pressure check should be made at 10″ Hg of vacuum in D-1, D-2, and L. Advance the throttle until the engine vacuum reading is 10″ Hg and check the control pressure regulation. Control

pressure should be 95–110 psi, as shown in the table.

CONTROL PRESSURE CHECK AT 3 INCHES OF VACUUM

Check control pressure at 3″ Hg of vacuum in D-1, D-2, and L. The control pressure should be 138–148 psi. Then move the selector lever to R. With the vacuum at 3″ Hg, the control pressure should be 213–227 psi, as shown in the table. *CAUTION: While making this pressure test, do not hold the throttle open for more than five seconds in each detent position. Between each test move the selector lever to neutral and run the engine at 1000 rpm for fifteen seconds to cool the converter.*

If the vacuum and pressure gauge readings are within specifications, the diaphragm unit and transmission control pressure regulating system are operating properly.

If the transmission control pressure is too low, too high, fails to increase with throttle opening, or is extremely erratic, use the procedure given under the following appropriate heading to resolve the problem.

CONTROL PRESSURE IS LOW AT ENGINE IDLE

If control pressure at engine idle is low in all selector lever positions, trouble other than the diaphragm unit is indicated. When the control pressure at engine idle is low in all ranges, check for excessive leakage in the front oil pump, case, and control valve body, or a sticking control pressure regulator valve.

CONTROL PRESSURE IS HIGH AT ENGINE IDLE

If the transmission control pressure at engine idle is too high in all ranges, the trouble may be in the diaphragm unit or its connecting vacuum tubes and hoses, throttle valve, or control rod.

With the engine idling, disconnect the hose from the diaphragm unit and check the engine manifold vacuum. Hold your thumb over the end of the hose and check for vacuum. If the engine speeds up when the hose is disconnected and slows down

Engine Speed or Manifold Vacuum	Throttle Position	Shift Selector Lever Position	*Control (Line) Pressure (psi)
Idle—Above 18 Inches of Vacuum	Closed	P,N,D1,D2,L	55-62
		R	55-96
17.5 to 16.5 Inches of Vacuum	As Required	D1,D2,L,R	Line Pressure Increase
10 Inches of Vacuum	As Required	D1,D2,L	95-110
3 Inches of Vacuum	As Required	D1,D2,L	138-148
		R	213-227

*Transmission oil at normal operating temperature.

Control pressures at zero output shaft speed.

C4 AUTOMATIC DUAL RANGE DIAGNOSIS GUIDE

Trouble Symptom	Items to Check		Probable Trouble Sources
	Transmission in Car	Transmission Out of Car	
Rough Initial Engagement in D1 or D2	K B W F E		A. Fluid Level
Rough Initial Engagement D2 Only	G J		B. Vacuum Diaphragm Unit or Tubes
1-2 or 2-3 Shift Points Incorrect	A B C D W E L		C. Manual Linkage
Rough 2-3 Shift	B F E		D. Governor
Engine Overspeeds on 2-3 Shift	B G W E F	r	E. Valve Body
No Shift Points	C D E J		F. Control Pressure Regulator Valve
No 2-3 Shift	C R D E	b r	G. Intermediate Band
No 3-1 Shift in D1	B E		H. Low-Reverse Band
No Forced Downshifts	L W E		I. Low-Reverse Servo
Runaway Engine on Forced Downshift	G F E J B	c	J. Intermediate Servo
Rough 3-2 or 3-1 Shift at Closed Throttle	K B E		K. Engine Idle Speed
Shifts 1-3 in D1 and D2	G J		L. Downshift Linkage
No Engine Braking in First Gear—Manual Low Range	H I		M. Converter Drain Plugs
Creeps Excessively in D1 or D2	K		N. Oil Pan Gasket, or Filler Tube
Slips or Chatters in First Gear, D1	A B W F E	a c i	O. Oil Cooler and Connections
Slips or Chatters in Second Gear	A B G W F E J	a c	P. Manual or Downshift Lever Shaft Seal
Slips or Chatters in R	A H W F E I	b c	Q. $\frac{1}{8}$-inch Pipe Plug in Side of Case
No Drive in D1 Only	C E	i	R. Perform Air-Pressure Check
No Drive in D2 Only	C		S. Extension Housing to Case Gaskets and Lockwashers
No Drive in R Only	C H I E R	b c	U. Extension Housing Rear Oil Seal
No Drive in D1, D2, or L	D W R	a	W. Perform Control Pressure Check
No Drive in Any Selector Lever Position	A C W F E R	c h	X. Speedometer Driven Gear Adapter Seal
Lockup in D2 Only	H I	i	a. Forward Clutch
Lockup in R Only		a g	b. Reverse-High Clutch
Parking Lock Binds or Does Not Hold	C	g	c. Leakage in Hydraulic System
Transmission Overheats	A O F	n	d. Front Pump
Maximum Speed Too Low, Poor Acceleration		n	g. Parking Linkage
Transmission Noisy in N	F	d	h. Planetary Assembly
Transmission Noisy in First, Second, and Reverse Gear	F	h d	i. Planetary One-Way Clutch
Transmission Noisy in P	F	d	j. Engine Rear Oil Seal
			m. Front Pump Oil Seal
Fluid Leak	M N O P Q S U X	j m p	n. Converter One-Way Clutch
			p. Front Pump to Case Gasket or Seal
			r. Reverse-High Clutch Piston Air Bleed Valve

Diagnosis guide for the Ford C-4 automatic transmission. The guide lists the most common trouble symptoms that may be found and gives the items that should be checked. Check in the above sequence for quickest results.

as your thumb is held against the end of the hose, the vacuum source is satisfactory.

Stop the engine, and remove the diaphragm unit and the diaphragm unit control rod. Inspect the control rod for a bent condition and for corrosion. Check the diaphragm unit for leakage with the distributor tester.

CONTROL PRESSURE DOES NOT INCREASE WITH VACUUM AT 17.5"–16.5" HG

When the control pressure is within specifications at engine idle, but does not increase, as the vacuum is decreased to the specified limits, first check the control rod between the vacuum unit and throttle valve for proper engagement. If the control rod is not assembled to the end of the throttle valve or vacuum unit, the valve cannot regulate throttle pressure to increase control pressure. Next check for a stuck secondary or primary throttle valve, pressure booster valve, or a stuck control pressure regulator valve.

If control pressure increases before or after vacuum is decreased from 17.5" to 16.5" Hg, check for a leaking diaphragm assembly, bent diaphragm can, or worn or bent control rod to the throttle valve.

CONTROL PRESSURE NOT WITHIN LIMITS AT 10" OR 3" HG OF VACUUM

If idle pressure and pressure point increase are within specifications but pressures at 10" or 3" Hg of vacuum are not within specifications in all ranges, excessive leakage, low pump capacity, or a restricted oil pan screen is indicated. If pressures are not within specifications for specific selector lever positions only, this indicates excessive leakage in the clutch or servo circuits used in those ranges.

When the control pressure is within specifications at engine idle, but not within specifications at the pressure rise point of 17.5" to 16.5" Hg of vacuum, at 10" Hg of vacuum, or at 3" Hg of vacuum, the vacuum diaphragm unit may need adjustment. The vacuum diaphragm assembly has an adjusting screw in the vacuum hose connecting tube. The inner end of the screw bears against a plate which in turn bears against the vacuum diaphragm spring. All readings slightly high or all readings slightly low may indicate the vacuum unit needs adjustment to correct a particular shift condition.

For example, if the pressure at 10" Hg of vacuum was 120 psi and the pressure at 3" Hg of vacuum was 170 psi, and upshifts and downshifts were harsh, a diaphragm adjustment to reduce the diaphragm assembly spring force would be required. If the pressure readings are low, and control pressure does not start to build up until vacuum drops to 15" Hg, an adjustment to increase diaphragm spring force is required.

To increase control pressure, turn the adjusting screw clockwise. To reduce control pressure, back the adjusting screw out by turning it counterclockwise. *NOTE: One complete turn of the adjusting screw (360°) will change idle line control pressure approximately 2–3 psi.* After the adjustment is made, install the vacuum line and make all the pressure checks as outlined in the table. *CAUTION: The diaphragm should not be adjusted to provide pressures below the ranges in the table, in order to change shift feel. To do so could result in soft or slipping shift points and damage to the transmission.*

STALL TEST

Start the engine to allow it to reach its normal temperature. Apply both the parking and service brakes while making the tests.

The stall test is made in D-2, D-1, L, or R, at full throttle to check engine performance, converter clutch operation or installation, and the holding ability of the forward clutch, reverse-high clutch, low-reverse band, and the gear train one-way clutch. *CAUTION: While making this test, do not hold the throttle open for more than five seconds at a time.* Then move the selector lever to Neutral and run the engine at 1000 rpm for about 15 seconds to cool the converter before making the next test. If the engine speed as recorded by the tachometer exceeds the maximum specified limits, release the accelerator immediately because clutch or band slippage is indicated.

STALL SPEED TOO HIGH

If the stall speed exceeds specifications, band or clutch slippage is indicated, depending on transmission selector lever position. Excessive engine rpm only in D-1, D-2, and L indicates forward clutch slippage. Excessive engine rpm only in R indicates either reverse-high clutch or low-reverse band slippage. Excessive engine rpm only in D-2 indicates gear train one-way clutch slippage.

STALL SPEED TOO LOW

When the stall test speeds are low and the engine is properly tuned, converter stator clutch problems are indicated. A road test must be performed to determine the exact cause of the trouble.

If the stall test speeds are 300 to 400 rpm below the specifications, and the car cruises properly but has very poor acceleration, the converter stator

Selector Lever Position	Clutch Applied	Band Applied	Engine Speed (rpm)	
			223-Six	289-V-8
D2	Forward	Intermediate		
D1	Forward	One-Way Clutch	1500-1700	1750-1950
L	Forward	Low-Reverse		
R	Reverse-High	Low-Reverse		

Stall speeds of the C-4 automatic transmission.

Axle Ratio	Automatic Shift Speeds (mph)								Manual Shift Speeds (mph)
	D1		D1 or D2		D1	D1 or D2	D1	D2	L
	1-2 Minimum Throttle	1-2 Maximum Throttle	2-3 Minimum Throttle	2-3 Maximum Throttle	3-1 Minimum Throttle	3-2 Maximum Throttle	2-1 or 3-1 Maximum Throttle	3-2 Minimum Throttle	2-1 Minimum Throttle
3.25:1 3.50:1	8-10	31-41	12-24	54-71	10 (max.)	64 (max.)	33 (max.)	10 (max.)	22 (max.)
3.00:1	9-11	36-44	14-25	64-76	11 (max.)	69 (max.)	35 (max.)	11 (max.)	23 (max.)

Shift points of the C-4 automatic transmission.

clutch is slipping. If the stall test speeds are 300 to 400 rpm below the specified values, and the car drags at cruising speeds and acceleration is poor, the stator clutch could be installed backwards.

When the stall test shows normal speeds, the acceleration is good, but the car drags at cruising speeds, the difficulty is due to a seized stator assembly. If the stator is defective, replace the converter.

INITIAL ENGAGEMENT CHECKS

Initial engagement checks are made to determine if initial band and clutch engagements are smooth. Run the engine until its normal operating temperature is reached. With the engine at the correct idle speed, shift the selector lever from N to D-2, D-1, L, and R. Observe the initial band and clutch engagements. Band and clutch engagements should be smooth in all positions. Rough band and clutch engagements in D-1, D-2, L, or R are caused by high engine idle speed or high control pressures.

SHIFT POINT CHECKS

Check the light throttle upshifts in D-1. The transmission should start in first gear, shift to second, and then shift to third, within the specified shift points.

While the transmission is in third gear, depress the accelerator pedal through the detent (to the floor). The transmission should shift from third to second or third to first, depending on the car speed.

Check the closed throttle downshift from third to first by coasting down from about 30 mph in third gear. The shift should occur within the limits specified in the table.

When the selector lever is at D-2, the transmission can operate only in second and third gears. Shift points for second to third and third to second are the same in both D-2 and D-1.

With the transmission in third gear and road speed over 30 mph, the transmission should shift to second gear when the selector lever is moved from D-2 or D-1 to L. When the same manual shift is made below about 20 mph, the transmission will shift from second or third to first. *NOTE:*

This check will determine if the governor pressure and shift control valves are functioning properly.

During the shift check operation, if the transmission does not shift within specifications or certain gear ratios cannot be obtained, refer to the Diagnosis Guide to resolve the problem.

AIR PRESSURE CHECKS

A "NO DRIVE" condition can exist, even with correct transmission fluid pressure, because of inoperative clutches or bands. The inoperative units can be located through a series of checks by substituting air pressure for the fluid pressure to determine the location of the malfunction.

When the selector lever is at D-2, a "NO DRIVE" condition may be caused by an inoperative forward clutch. A "NO DRIVE" condition at D-1 may be caused by an inoperative forward clutch or one-way clutch. When there is no drive in L, the difficulty could be caused by improper functioning of the forward clutch or low-reverse band and the one-way clutch. Failure to drive in reverse range could be caused by a malfunction of the reverse-high clutch or low-reverse band. Erratic shifts

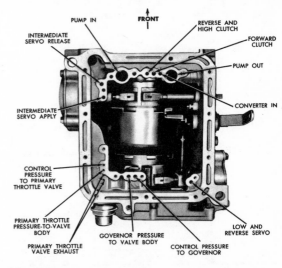

Identification of passageways in the case for introducing air for checking band and clutch application.

could be caused by a stuck governor valve.

To make the air pressure checks, loosen the oil pan bolts and lower one edge of the oil pan to drain the transmission fluid. Remove the oil pan and the control valve body assembly. The inoperative units can be located by introducing air pressure into the transmission case passages leading to the clutches, servos, and governor.

Forward Clutch

Apply air pressure to the transmission case forward clutch passage. A dull thud can be heard when the clutch piston is applied. If no noise is heard, place the finger tips on the input shell and again apply air pressure to the forward clutch passage. Movement of the piston can be felt as the clutch is applied.

Governor

Apply air pressure to the control-pressure-to-governor passage and listen for a sharp clicking or whistling noise. The noise indicates governor valve movement.

Reverse-High Clutch

Apply air pressure to the reverse-high clutch passage. A dull thud indicates that the reverse-high clutch piston has moved to the applied position. If no noise is heard, place the finger tips on the clutch drum and again apply air pressure to detect movement of the piston.

Intermediate Servo

Hold the air nozzle in the intermediate servo apply passage. Operation of the servo is indicated by a tightening of the intermediate band around the drum. Continue to apply air pressure to the intermediate servo apply passage and introduce air pressure into the intermediate servo release passage. The intermediate servo should release the band against the apply pressure.

Low-Reverse

Apply air pressure to the low-reverse apply passage. The low-reverse band should tighten around the drum if the servo is operating properly. If the servos do not operate, disassemble, clean, and inspect them to locate the source of the trouble. If air pressure applied to either of the clutch passages

CONTROL PRESSURE AT ZERO OUTPUT SHAFT SPEED

Engine Speed or Manifold Vacuum	Throttle Position	Shift Selector Lever Position	* Control (Line) Pressure (psi)
Idle- Above 18 Inches of Vacuum	Closed	P, N, D1, D2	60 - 66
		L, R	60 - 102
17.5 to 16.5 Inches of Vacuum	As Required	D1, D2	Line Pressure Increase
10 Inches of Vacuum	As Required	D1, D2	99 - 114
3 Inches of Vacuum	As Required	D1, D2	142 - 152
		L, R	218 - 232

The control pressures are different for the special Fairlane high-performance engine as discussed in the text.

fails to operate a clutch or operates both clutches at once, remove and, with air pressure, check the fluid passages in the case and front pump to detect obstructions. If the passages are clear, remove the clutch assemblies, and clean and inspect the malfunctioning clutch to locate the trouble.

SPECIAL CONTROL VALVE BODY

1964 Fairlane with 289 cu. in., 4 Bbl. carburetor high-performance engine

A special control valve body is used on these engines to provide maximum stall pressures through all ranges, rather than just in reverse. With this valve body, the following control pressure test specifications apply. The stall engine test specifications are 1750–1950 rpm.

TROUBLESHOOTING A POWERGLIDE (CAST IRON CASE) TRANSMISSION

APPLICATION: Chevrolet through 1962

Basic Pressure Tests. The following seven basic pressure checks are used for diagnosis. They should be made only on a thoroughly warmed transmission and with the engine idling speed set to 425 rpm in the "D" range.

The pressure gauge hose connection should be installed at the low servo apply (main line), clutch (release side of the low servo), throttle valve, and governor pressure test points. The gauge lines can be run into the driving compartment by pushing aside the mast jacket seal. *CAUTION: Stall tests are not recommended.*

Axle Ratio	Automatic Shift Speeds (mph)								Manual Shift Speeds (mph)
	D1		D1 or D2		D1	D1 or D2	D1	D2	L
	1-2 Minimum Throttle	1-2 Maximum Throttle	2-3 Minimum Throttle	2-3 Maximum Throttle	3-1 Minimum Throttle	3-2 Maximum Throttle	2-1 or 3-1 Maximum Throttle	3-2 Minimum Throttle	2-1 Minimum Throttle
3.89:1	7-9	35-38	7-20	64-73	8 (Max)	68 (Max)	36 (Max)	8 (Max)	22 (Max)
3.50:1	7-9	42-50	8-23	71-81	9 (Max)	75 (Max)	40 (Max)	9 (Max)	24 (Max)

Shift points of the special Fairlane with the high-performance engine.

Wide-Open Throttle Upshift Pressure Check. A wide-open throttle upshift should occur at 82–90 psi on a car with a V-8 engine, or at 68–74 psi on a car with a 6-cylinder engine as indicated on the low servo apply (main line) gauge. After the shift, the pressures on both the low servo apply and the high clutch gauges should register the same. If the pressures are correct and clutch slippage is felt, mechanical trouble in the clutch is indicated. If high clutch pressure is 5 psi lower than specifications, check for a leak in the high clutch line between the low-and-drive valve body and the high clutch.

Idle Pressure in "Drive" Range. In addition to the pressure gauges, a vacuum gauge is required for this check. With the parking brake applied and the shift selector lever in the "DRIVE" position, adjust the engine speed until a steady 16" Hg is indicated on the vacuum gauge. Low servo apply (main line) pressure should be 60–65 psi with a V-8 engine or 55–65 psi with a 6-cylinder engine. If the pressures are not within this range, the following items should be checked for oil circuit leakage: (1) Pressure regulator valve stuck. (2) Vacuum modulator valve stuck. (3) Booster valve stuck. (4) Leak at the low servo piston ring (between ring and bore). (5) Leak at the low servo piston rod (between the rod and bore). (6) Leak at the valve body-to-case gasket. (7) Leak between the valve body and the housing. (8) Front pump clearances excessive. (9) Leak at the low drive valve body (check gasket and shifter valve). (10) Check the passages in the transmission housing for porosity. (11) Loose suction screen connection.

Manual "Low" Range Pressure Check. Connect a tachometer, place the selector lever in "LOW" range, and adjust the engine speed to 1000 rpm with the car stationary. The low servo apply (main line) pressure should be 114–127 psi on cars with a V-8 engine or 70–80 psi on cars with a 6-cylinder engine. Pressures not within this range can be caused by the following: (1) Partially plugged oil suction screen. (2) Broken or damaged ring in low servo. (3) Pressure regulator valve stuck. (4) Leak at the valve body-to-case gasket. (5) Leak between the valve body and housing. (6) Leak at the servo center. (7) Excessive front pump clearances.

Drive Range Overrun (Coast) Pressure. With the car coasting in "DRIVE" range at 20–25 mph and the engine vacuum at about 20" Hg, the low servo apply (main line) pressure should be 47–53 psi for both engines.

Throttle Valve and Governor Pressure Checks. Readings for throttle valve pressure will range from 0–63 psi on a car with a V-8 engine or 0–50 on a car with a 6-cylinder engine, depending on accelerator position. Improper TV pressure is usually the result of trouble in the low-and-drive valve body, provided that the TV linkage is properly adjusted. Governor pressure is relative to the transmission output shaft speed and can be checked in terms of mph by referring to the following chart:

GOVERNOR PRESSURE CHART

Car Speed (mph)	Governor Pressure (psi)
5	2–4
10	8½–13
15	21–27½
20	31½–34½
25	35½–40
30	41–46
35	47½–53½
40	55–62
45	63½–71½
50	73½–82
55	84–93½
60	95½–106

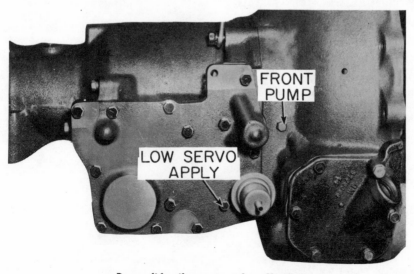

Powerglide oil pressure take-off points.

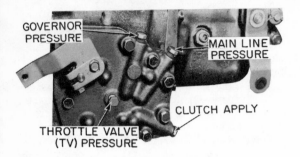

Oil pressure take-off points on the left side of the transmission.

If pressures are not within specified limits, the governor assembly should be checked. Throttle valve and governor pressure checks are generally made in conjunction with a shift pattern test. If improper upshifts or downshifts occur, check the TV linkage, then the governor pressure as previously described, and then the TV pressures.

Reverse Pressure Check. With the parking brake applied, place the selector lever in "REVERSE" and adjust the idle speed to 1000 rpm. The pressure reading on the low servo apply (main line) gauge should be 240–275 psi on cars with a V-8 engine or 167–191 psi on cars with a 6-cylinder engine. If the pressures are within limits but operation in reverse is faulty, the reverse band requires adjustment or replacement. If the pressure is below limits, the following items should be checked: (1) Partially plugged oil suction screen. (2) Broken or damaged reverse servo piston ring. (3) Pressure regulator valve or booster valve stuck. (4) Leak at the valve body-to-case gasket. (5) Front pump clearances excessive. (6) Leak between the piston rod and bore.

POWERGLIDE TROUBLESHOOTING CHART

TROUBLES & CAUSES

1. **Closed throttle downshift clunk**
   1a. High engine idle speed
   1b. Downshift timing valve malfunction
   1c. High main line pressure. Check the following:
      1. Vacuum hose to modulator leaking
      2. Modulator diaphragm ruptured
      3. Sticking valves: pressure regulator booster valve, pressure regulator valve, or modulator valve

2. **Clutch failure**
   2a. Low band adjusting screw backed off more than specified for low servo piston used.
   2b. Improper nesting of clutch plates on assembly. The "O" marks on the steel plates must all face the same direction in the pack.
   2c. Improper order of assembly. A steel plate must be installed first, alternating with the four composition plates, ending with a steel plate (five steel plates used).

2d. Operation with low oil level
2e. Abnormal high speed upshift. This can be caused by improper governor action or by driver abuse in which the transmission is operated at high speed in manual "LOW" range.
2f. Overspeeding in reverse on ice, snow, or in mud. When the transmission is in reverse the clutch plates are rotating in opposite directions, the drive plates are revolving at 44 times the driven plates; therefore, any slight clutch drag would soon burn out the unit.
2g. Improperly drilled orifice in low-and-drive valve body

3. **Clutch hydraulic tests**
   3a. To test the hydraulic action of the clutch, connect a pressure gauge to the low servo apply (main line) and the high clutch (release side of the low servo) test points. With the selector lever in "DRIVE," check for slow build-up of pressure on the gauge connected to the high clutch which would indicate restriction in the high clutch apply orifice in the low drive valve body, which would result in clutch slippage.
   3b. With the selector lever in "LOW," check for pressure on the gauge connected to the high clutch. If any pressure is shown, leakage past the low servo piston ring is indicated which would result in partial application of the clutch.

4. **Difficulty in shifting from drive to low and back again**
   4a. This trouble can be caused by an improperly drilled high clutch feed orifice in the low-drive valve body. A restriction would result in slow application of the clutch.

5. **Runaway engine**
   5a. Malfunction in the pressure regulation system
   5b. Sump baffle out of place

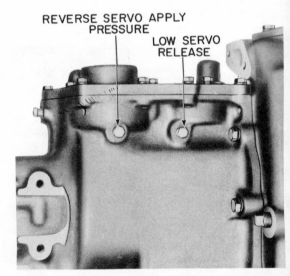

Oil pressure take-off points on the bottom of the Powerglide automatic transmission.

TROUBLESHOOTING A POWERGLIDE (ALUMINUM CASE) AUTOMATIC TRANSMISSION

APPLICATION: Chevrolet since 1962

Basic Pressure Tests. Five pressure tests are used for diagnosis on a thoroughly warmed power plant. Stall-tests are not recommended. Pressure gauge hose connections should be made at the servo apply (main line) and reverse pressure test points.

WIDE-OPEN THROTTLE UPSHIFT PRESSURE TEST. Wide-open throttle upshift should occur at 93–103 psi for the 327 cu. in. engine, at 95–105 psi for the 283 cu. in. engine, and at 98–108 psi for the 4- and 6-cyl. engines.

IDLE PRESSURE IN DRIVE RANGE. With the shift selector lever in DRIVE and the parking brake firmly applied, the main line (servo apply) pressure should be 60–70 psi at 16" Hg of vacuum and 89–99 psi at 10" Hg of vacuum. If the pressures are not within specifications, the following items are possible sources of trouble: (1) Pressure regulator valve stuck. (2) Vacuum modulator valve stuck. (3) Hydraulic modulator valve stuck. (4) Leak at the low servo piston ring (between the ring and the bore). (5) Leak at the low servo piston rod (between the rod and the bore). (6) Leak at the valve body-to-case gasket. (7) Leak at the valve body gaskets. (8) Excessive front pump clearances. (9) Porosity in the case passages.

MANUAL LOW RANGE PRESSURE TEST. Connect a tachometer, apply the parking brake, place the selector lever in LOW range, and adjust the engine speed to 1000 rpm. With the car stationary, the servo apply (main line) pressure should be 126–134 psi. If the pressure is not within specifications, the following items are possible sources of trouble: (1) Partially plugged oil suction screen. (2) Broken ring in the low servo. (3) Pressure regulator valve stuck. (4) Leak at the valve body-to-case gasket. (5) Leak between the valve body gaskets. (6) Leak at the servo center. (7) Excessive front pump clearances.

DRIVE RANGE OVERRUN (COAST) PRESSURE TEST. With the vehicle coasting in the DRIVE range at 20–25 mph and with the engine vacuum at 20" Hg, the servo apply (main line) pressure should be 48–54 psi.

Oil pressure testing point on the right side of the aluminum case Powerglide automatic transmission.

POWERGLIDE TROUBLESHOOTING CHART

TROUBLES & CAUSES

1. **No drive in any selector position**
   1a. Low oil level
   1b. Clogged oil suction screen
   1c. Defective pressure regulator valve
   1d. Front pump defective
   1e. Input shaft broken
   1f. Front pump priming valve stuck
2. **Engine speed flares on standstill starts, but acceleration lags**
   2a. Low band partially applied because of: (a) low oil level, (b) clogged oil suction screen, (c) improper band adjustment, (d) servo apply passage blocked, (e) servo piston ring broken or leaking, (f) band facing worn, (g) low band apply linkage disengaged or broken, (h) converter stator not holding
3. **Engine speed flares on upshifts**
   3a. Low oil level
   3b. Improper band adjustment
   3c. Clogged oil suction screen
   3d. High clutch partially applied; blocked feed orifice
   3e. High clutch plates worn
   3f. High clutch seals leaking
   3g. High clutch piston hung up
   3h. High clutch drum relief ball not seating
   3i. Vacuum modulator line plugged
4. **Transmission will not upshift**
   4a. Low band not releasing, probably due to:

CHEVROLET ALUMINUM CASE POWERGLIDE SHIFT POINTS

Engine	230 L-6		283 V-8		327 V-8		327 V-8 Hi-Perf.	
Throttle Position	Up	Down	Up	Down	Up	Down	Up	Down
Closed	14–18	13–17	14–18	13–17	14–16	11–15	12–15	10–15
Detent touch	43–50	28–33	47–54	16–22	48–58	16–19	49–60	14–17
Through detent	51–57	47–54	55–62	53–59	59–65	56–61	59–66	57–62

CHEVY II ALUMINUM CASE POWERGLIDE SHIFT POINTS

	L-4 and L-6 Engines	
	Up	Down
Closed	12–16	12–15
Detent touch	39–45	25–30
Through detent	45–51	42–48

(a) stuck low-drive valve, (b) defective governor, (c) no rear pump output caused by stuck priming valve, sheared drive pin, or defective pump, (d) throttle valve stuck or maladjusted, (e) maladjusted manual valve lever

5. Upshifts harsh
5a. Incorrect carburetor-to-transmission TV rod adjustment
5b. Improper low band adjustment
5c. Vacuum modulator line broken or disconnected
5d. Vacuum modulator diaphragm leaking
5e. Vacuum modulator valve stuck
5f. Hydraulic modulator valve stuck

6. Closed throttle (coast) downshifts harsh
6a. Improper band adjustment
6b. High engine idle speed
6c. Downshift timing valve defective
6d. High main line pressure. Check: (a) vacuum modulator line broken or disconnected, (b) modulator diaphragm ruptured, (c) sticking hydraulic modulator valve, pressure regulator valve, or vacuum modulator valve

7. Will not downshift
7a. Sticking low-drive shift valve
7b. Low-drive shift plug stuck
7c. High governor pressure
7d. Low TV pressure

8. Clutch failure; burned plates
8a. Low band adjusting screw backed off more than specified
8b. Improper order of clutch plate assembly
8c. Extended operation with low oil level
8d. Clutch drum relief ball stuck
8e. Abnormally high speed upshift: (a) improper governor action, (b) transmission operated at high speed in manual LOW

9. Car creeps excessively in DRIVE
9a. Idle speed too high

10. Car creeps in NEUTRAL
10a. Incorrect manual valve lever adjustment
10b. High clutch or low band not releasing

11. No drive in REVERSE
11a. Incorrect manual valve lever adjustment
11b. Reverse clutch piston stuck
11c. Reverse clutch plates worn
11d. Reverse clutch leaking excessively
11e. Blocked reverse clutch apply orifice

12. Improper shift points
12a. Incorrectly adjusted carburetor-to-transmission linkage
12b. Incorrectly adjusted throttle valve
12c. Governor defective
12d. Rear pump priming valve stuck

13. Unable to push-start
13a. Rear pump drive gear not engaged with drive pin on output shaft
13b. Drive pin sheared off
13c. Rear pump priming valve not sealing

14. Oil leaks
14a. Transmission case and extension: (a) extension oil seal, (b) shifter shaft oil seal, (c) speedometer driven gear fitting, (d) pressure taps, (e) oil cooler pipe connections, (f) vacuum modulator assembly and case. *NOTE*: *A very smoky exhaust indicates a ruptured vacuum modulator diaphragm.*
14b. Transmission oil pan gasket
14c. Converter cover pan: (a) front pump attaching bolts, (b) front pump seal ring, (c) front pump oil seal, (d) oil drain in front pump plugged, (e) porosity in transmission case

15. Oil forced out of filler tube
15a. Oil level too high; aeration and foaming caused by planet carrier running in oil
15b. Water in oil
15c. Leak in pump suction circuits

TROUBLESHOOTING A TURBOGLIDE TRANSMISSION

APPLICATION: Chevrolet through 1962

Preliminary Checks. Before making any tests, it is important that the engine is in tune, that the oil level is correct, and that the engine and transmission are warmed to proper operating temperature. A 5-mile trip with starts and stops will warm the equipment to its normal operating temperature.

The Chevrolet Motor Company does not recommend a stall-test because damage to the transmission may result. Instead, they suggest a road test with a pressure gauge, vacuum gauge, and a tachometer connected so that all are visible from the driver's seat.

Road Test. With the selector lever in the D range and the car speed at 30 mph, push the accelerator to a wide-open position. The engine speed should increase 700 to 900 rpm if the stator is functioning properly. The pressure should rise to 190–210 psi with a 3" Hg reading on the vacuum gauge. At a road speed of 45 mph in the D range, take your foot off the throttle. The pressure gauge should drop to 80–90 psi with 18–25" Hg of vacuum.

Shop Tests. Five air checks can be made to the transmission which will be of value in determining the exact cause of trouble before the transmission is disassembled. It also is the best way to locate defective seals, which might leak unless replaced during the repair process.

To make the air tests, raise the car on a hoist, drain the oil, remove the transmission underpan,

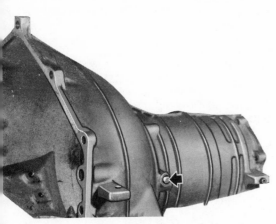

Pressure testing point on the left side of the Turbo-glide automatic transmission.

the oil pan, and the main valve body. Special tubes must be installed in the forward clutch and grade retarder apply ports to make the tests.

REVERSE CLUTCH. Apply air to the reverse clutch port. Check to see that the reverse piston applies and listen for air leaks. If the piston does not apply, determine whether the front pump-to-transmission case gasket is incorrectly positioned, which can block the oil passages, or if the reverse piston is seized. If air leaks are heard, check for a damaged front pump-to-transmission case gasket, or for damaged seals in the reverse piston circuit.

STATOR PISTON. Apply air to the stator piston port and listen for air leaks. If leaks are detected, check for a mispositioned or damaged front pump-to-transmission case gasket, broken or warped seal rings on the second turbine shaft, or a defective stator piston seal.

NEUTRAL CLUTCH. Apply air to the neutral clutch port and listen for an application of the clutch and for air leaks. If no clutch application is heard, determine if the front pump-to-transmission case gasket is incorrectly positioned, which can block the oil passages. If not, you will have to disassemble the neutral clutch to determine the exact cause. If air leaks are heard, possible causes are: a torn or distorted front pump-to-transmission case gasket, warped or broken oil seal rings on the neutral clutch piston, or the clutch hub check ball not seating.

FORWARD CLUTCH. Apply air pressure to the forward clutch tube and see if the clutch applies. Listen for air leaks. Failure of the clutch to apply can be caused by a wedged forward piston, probably due to a cocked piston "O" ring. Blockage of the pressure passage in the piston support could also prevent clutch application. If air leaks are heard, check the "O" ring seals on the oil pressure tube in the forward clutch port and the forward piston-to-support seals.

GRADE RETARDER PISTON. Apply air to the grade retarder port. Check the application of the piston

by watching for movement of the grade retarder reaction plate. If it doesn't move, check for cocked "O" ring seals on the brake piston or a blocked pressure passage in the piston support. Leakage can occur only at the oil pressure tube "O" ring seal or at the brake piston "O" ring seals.

TURBOGLIDE TRANSMISSION TROUBLE-SHOOTING CHART

TROUBLES & CAUSES

1. **No drive in any selector position, cannot load engine**
   1a. Low oil level
   1b. Front pump defective or assembled backward
   1c. Front pump priming ball not seating
   1d. Defective converter pump
2. **No drive except in Grade Retard, cannot load engine**
   2a. Both overrun clutches assembled backward
3. **No drive except in Grade Retard and Reverse, cannot load engine in Drive**
   3a. Outer overrun clutch assembled backward
   3b. Forward and neutral clutch not applied due to severe leakage in forward clutch hydraulic circuit
4. **Drive is poor at low speeds, no Reverse, Grade Retard normal**
   4a. Inner overrun clutch assembled backward
   4b. Stator overrun clutch not holding
5. **Car drives very slightly in Neutral, Reverse normal**
   5a. Neutral clutch not released
6. **Car drives normal in Neutral and Drive at low speeds, no Reverse**
   6a. Forward clutch not released
7. **Transmission will not shift to performance stator angle**
   7a. Stator control linkage out of adjustment

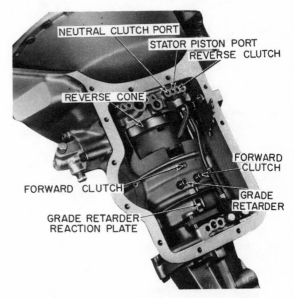

Oil passageway identification for introduction of air to operate the servos and clutches.

7b. Converter charging pressure is low because leakage reduces line pressure enough to cause pressure regulator valve to shut off converter "in" line or there is leakage in the converter circuit

7c. Discharge orifice in transfer plate plugged

7d. Broken or leaking seal rings on second turbine shaft. Damage to front ring allows converter "out" pressure to leak to stator passage. Damage to middle ring allows neutral pressure to leak to converter "out" passage

8. Unable to push start

8a. Rear oil pump drive pin broken or missing

9. Clutch slippage on wide-open throttle starts

9a. Low oil pressure due to leakage. Especially check forward pressure tube "O" ring

9b. Mechanical interference which will prevent forward piston from fully applying

9c. Forward clutch facing failure

9d. Front pump priming ball seating poorly causing excessive leakage and low oil pressure

10. Grade Retard slow to apply

10a. Control linkage out of adjustment, preventing manual valve getting into Grade Retard position

10b. Low pressure resulting from leakage. Check pressure tube "O" ring seals

10c. Mechanical interference of Grade Retard piston

10d. Glazed Grade Retard plates

11. No Drive, Reverse normal, no Grade Retard

11a. Reverse clutch not disengaged

12. Grade Retard brakes violently

12a. Vacuum hose disconnected

12b. Vacuum modulator diaphragm ruptured or hose disconnected

12c. Forward clutch not disengaged

13. Shifts from standstill very slowly

13a. Check linkage to ascertain that shift lever is positioned by transmission detents

13b. Leakage in hydraulic system. Check pressure tube "O" rings and other seals and gaskets

13c. Front pump priming ball seating poorly

13d. Front pump side clearance excessive

14. Shifts from standstill very fast and harsh

14a. Vacuum modulator diaphragm ruptured

14b. Vacuum hose disconnected

14c. Excessively high idle speed

14d. Defective neutral accumulator spring

15. Excess vibration in Neutral

15a. Converter and flywheel not in proper alignment

TROUBLESHOOTING A TWIN-TURBINE TRANSMISSION

APPLICATION: Buick through 1963

Road Test. After the transmission has been warmed to normal operating temperature, test its operation in all ranges, making tests on steep grades as well as on level roads. While in DIRECT DRIVE, test the shifting of the two-piston stator by pressing on the accelerator pedal to the floorboard a few times. Engine speed should increase and should be accompanied by increased acceleration, which indicates that the stator has shifted to the high-angle position.

Test the operation when shifting between LOW and DIRECT DRIVE under load. Also check the operation in DIRECT DRIVE after extended operation in REVERSE. Check for abnormal slip or over-run of the engine on low-speed acceleration. With the car stopped on level ground and the brakes released, check for creep when the engine is accelerated with the transmission in NEUTRAL. Check for abnormal creep with the engine idling and the transmission in each of the driving ranges.

Place the transmission in DIRECT DRIVE and firmly apply the brakes. Snap the throttle open to obtain an engine speed of about 1400 rpm, and then immediately release the accelerator pedal. If the engine returns to idle too slowly, or returns too fast so that it stalls or idles unevenly, the throttle linkage and dashpot are improperly adjusted. Rough operation on idle after slow deceleration indicates the need for an engine tune-up.

During all tests be alert for any unusual or abnormal noises. Carefully note the range, speed, and other conditions under which the noise appears.

Shop Tests. After the road test, a number of shop tests can be made to isolate the trouble:

1. Check the oil level. Excessive oil consumption indicates leaking seals.

2. Check the manual control linkage, especially in

Buick Twin-Turbine automatic transmission oil pressure testing points.

cases of improper operation in one or more ranges.

3. Check the engine and transmission mountings for loose bolts and soft condition of the rubber.

4. Check the oil pressures in the hydraulic control system as follows:

4a. Remove the pipe plug and connect an oil pressure gauge to each of the following points in turn: (a) front oil pump; (b) high or low accumulator; and (c) stator.

4b. Run the engine at 500 rpm and test the pump and accumulator pressures in LOW, DRIVE, and REVERSE.

4c. Test the front oil pump in all ranges.

4d. Test the high accumulator in DRIVE only.

4e. Test the low accumulator in LOW only.

4f. Repeat the tests at 1000 and 1800 rpm in LOW and DRIVE only.

The following pressures should be obtained on the above tests:

Engine (rpm)	Trans. Range	Front Pump	Accum- ulator	Stator (min.)
500	Low	120	115	—
	Drive	90	80	10
	Reverse	120	—	—
1000	Low	180	175	—
	Drive	90	85	70
1800	Low	180	175	—
	Drive	90	85	75

HYDRAULIC PRESSURE TROUBLESHOOTING CHART

TROUBLES & CAUSES

1. **Low or erratic oil pump pressure**
   1a. Air leaking into the pump suction line
   1b. Faulty pressure regulator valve operation
   1c. Excessive clearance in oil pump

2. **Very low accumulator pressure**
   2a. External or internal leak past the accumulator body gasket
   2b. Leak between the accumulator and the clutch (if over 10 psi difference between front pump and accumulator and if the high accumulator pressure is low)
   2c. Leak between the accumulator and the low servo (if low accumulator pressure is low)
   2d. Metering orifice in accumulator restricted or plugged

3. **Low pressure at high accumulator**
   3a. Leak in the stator oil circuit. To check this out, disconnect the control rod from the lever on the accumulator, make certain that the lever is properly positioned and tight on the valve crank, and then raise the lever against its stop while noting the gauge reading. A rise in pressure indicates a leak in the stator control circuit.

TWIN-TURBINE TRANSMISSION TROUBLESHOOTING CHART

TROUBLES & CAUSES

1. **Engine stalls during deceleration**
   1a. Improper adjustment of dashpot
   1b. Engine needs tuning

2. **Oil foams from breather**
   2a. Transmission overfull
   2b. Water in transmission from leaking oil cooler
   2c. Air leak into hydraulic system at rear oil pump gaskets

3. **Car will not move in any range—rear wheels free**
   3a. Front pump loses prime due to excessive clearances
   3b. If condition exists only after extended operation in REVERSE, air is leaking into pump suction line and there is excessive clearance at front pump

4. **Car will not move in any range—rear wheels locked**
   4a. Parking lock engaged or parking brake applied
   4b. Lock up due to broken part in rear axle or transmission

5. **Car will not move in DIRECT DRIVE only**
   5a. If front oil pump and high accumulator pressures are OK, inspect the clutch assembly
   5b. If front oil pump pressure is OK but high accumulator pressure is low, and accumulator body gasket is not leaking internally, inspect for leaks in the reaction flange gasket. If the gasket is satisfactory, inspect the clutch piston outer seal and ball check, also the oil sealing rings on the hub of the reaction shaft flange and low drum

6. **Car will not move in REVERSE only**
   6a. Reverse servo inoperative
   6b. Band improperly adjusted or band operating strut out of position

7. **Slips in all ranges**
   7a. Low oil level
   7b. Manual control linkage improperly adjusted
   7c. If front oil pump pressure is low, remove and inspect the pressure regulator valve and all valve and servo body gaskets. Also inspect the reaction shaft flange gaskets for leaks

8. **Slips in DIRECT DRIVE only**
   8a. Leak at high accumulator gasket
   8b. Manual control linkage improperly adjusted
   8c. If above items are OK, remove and inspect the clutch plates, sealing rings, and clutch piston. Also inspect the ball check in the piston for free operation

9. **Slips in LOW only**
   9a. Manual control linkage improperly adjusted
   9b. Low band improperly adjusted
   9c. If pressure at low accumulator is low, check for leak at accumulator body gasket. If gasket is OK, remove the valve and servo body to check for gasket leaks and also the condition of the low servo piston seal
   9d. Low band and drum scored or worn

10. **Slips in REVERSE only**
    10a. Manual control linkage improperly adjusted
    10b. Reverse band improperly adjusted

10c. If front oil pump pressure is low, remove the valve and servo body and check for gasket leaks and also the condition of the reverse servo piston seal

10d. Reverse band and ring gear scored or worn

11. Car creeps forward in NEUTRAL

11a. Manual control linkage improperly adjusted

11b. Low servo piston hanging up

11c. Remove the clutch and inspect for sticking, warped, or improperly assembled clutch plates. Check to see that the "dish" of each steel plate is in the same direction. If creep occurs at approximately 2500 rpm, inspect the ball checks at the vents in the clutch piston and reaction shaft flange

12. Car creeps forward in REVERSE or backward in LOW

12a. Manual control linkage improperly adjusted

13. LOW to DIRECT shift abnormally rough, or slip occurs

13a. Check accumulator body gasket if high accumulator pressure is low

13b. Accumulator piston sticking (top land of piston must be fully visible through top port in body)

13c. Leak in valve and servo body gaskets, especially if the accumulator gaskets are OK

13d. Low band improperly adjusted

13e. Binding or worn clutch plates

14. Excessive chatter or "clunk" when starting in LOW or REVERSE

14a. Engine and transmission mountings loose

14b. Low or reverse band improperly adjusted

14c. Direct drive clutch dragging

14d. Excessive wear in reverse ring gear bushing

15. Hard shifting out of PARKING

15a. Binding of transmission shift rod in shift idler lever

16. Noises

16a. A hum or whine in NEUTRAL or PARKING is normal since all planetary gears are rotating freely

16b. Buzzing noise can be caused by a low oil level or by the front pump delivery check valve seating on the edge of the gasket between the valve and servo bodies

16c. Buzzing noise in PARKING or NEUTRAL may be caused by excessive clearance in the pressure regulator valve

16d. Clicking noise in all ranges may be caused by a foreign object in the converter

16e. Clicking noise only when car is in motion may be caused by the parking lock pawl contacting the ratchet wheel due to improper linkage adjustment

16f. Abnormal hum or whine in all ranges may be caused by excessive clearances in the front oil pump. Noise in the front oil pump will diminish above 45 mph

16g. Abnormal hum or whine in all ranges except DIRECT DRIVE may be caused by worn planetary gear train

16h. Squealing or screeching immediately following installation of front oil pump parts indicates that the driving gear has been installed backward. This condition must be corrected immediately, otherwise severe damage will result

16i. Whistling noise which occurs during low speed acceleration in DRIVE, LOW, and REVERSE, accompanied by unsatisfactory transmission performance, indicates cavitation of oil due to incomplete filling of the torque converter. It can be caused by a restriction in the passages leading to the converter or in the passages in the reaction shaft flange

16j. Whistling noise which occurs during low speed acceleration in DRIVE, LOW, and REVERSE, but with otherwise satisfactory transmission performance, may be caused by thin, weak, or cracked turbine vanes, or vanes which are bent over at the exit edge

TROUBLESHOOTING THE TURBINE 300 AUTOMATIC TRANSMISSION

APPLICATION: Buick, Buick Special, Oldsmobile and Tempest, since 1964

PRESSURE CHECKS

Pressure checks are useful to determine whether the trouble is mechanical or hydraulic in nature. All pressure checks can be made by raising the rear wheels about 5" from the floor and connecting a 250 psi gauge into the main line pressure tap on the right side of the case. With a thoroughly warmed transmission, and the oil level up to the full mark, make sure that the vacuum line connections are tight, and then check the linkage adjustment as discussed at the end of the overhaul section.

Mainline pressure will vary from one transmission to another, but the following apply in general to all models. (1) Line pressure should increase as engine manifold vacuum decreases. (2) Line pressure should decrease as car speed increases (at a constant manifold vacuum). The decrease should be about 13 psi as the speed increases from 40–60 mph. (3) Reverse pressure should be about 90 psi at idle and over 200 psi at stall. *CAUTION: Do not operate at stall conditions for longer than necessary to obtain a gauge reading.* (4) Line pressure at wide-open throttle upshift should be about 85–100 psi. (5) Mainline pressure should be about 140–160 psi in DRIVE range. (6) In LOW range the pressure should not drop below 90 psi.

TURBINE 300 TROUBLESHOOTING CHART

TROUBLES AND CAUSES

1. No drive in any selector position; cannot load the engine

1a. Low oil level

1b. Clogged oil strainer screen or suction pipe loose

1c. Defective pressure regulator valve

1d. Front pump defective

1e. Input shaft broken

2. Engine speed flares on standstill starts, but acceleration lags

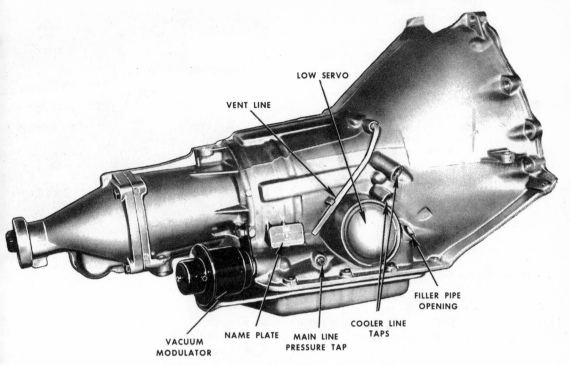

LOW SERVO

VENT LINE

FILLER PIPE OPENING

COOLER LINE TAPS

VACUUM MODULATOR

NAME PLATE

MAIN LINE PRESSURE TAP

The right side of the Turbine 300 automatic transmission showing the modulator and main line pressure tap.

2a. Low oil level
2b. Clogged oil strainer screen
2c. Servo piston seal leaking
2d. Band facing worn
2e. Low band apply struts disengaged or broken

3. Engine speed flares on upshifts
3a. Low oil level
3b. Improper band adjustment
3c. Clogged oil strainer screen
3d. Forward clutch partially applied
3e. Forward clutch plates worn
3f. Forward clutch piston hanging up
3g. Forward clutch drum relief ball not sealing
3h. Vacuum modulator diaphragm leaks

4. Harsh upshifts
4a. Vacuum modulator line broken or disconnected
4b. Vacuum modulator diaphragm leaks
4c. Vacuum modulator valve stuck

5. Harsh closed-throttle (coast) downshift
5a. Low band improperly adjusted
5b. High engine idle speed
5c. Downshift timing valve malfunction
5d. High main line pressure due to: (a) vacuum modulator line broken or disconnected, (b) modulator diaphragm ruptured, and (c) sticking pressure regulator coast valve, pressure regulator valve, or vacuum modulator valve

6. Clutch failure
6a. Low band adjusting screw backed off more than specified
6b. Improper order of clutch plate assembly
6c. Extended operation with low oil level
6d. Forward clutch drum relief ball stuck

7. Car creeps excessively in DRIVE
7a. Idle speed too high

7b. Closed-throttle stator switch improperly adjusted

8. No upshift below 50 mph (upshifts above)
8a. Vacuum line disconnected or leaking (causes abnormally high line pressure)
8b. Failure of modulator diaphragm (causes excessive exhaust smoke)
8c. Downshift solenoid stuck in downshift position
8d. Downshift switch shorted or stuck
8e. Modulator valve stuck (causes erratic line pressure)

9. No forced downshift above 15 mph
9a. Defective downshift switch
9b. Downshift solenoid stuck closed
9c. Detent valve stuck

10. No upshift at any speed
10a. Governor stuck (results in normal pressure at 0 mph, but does not decrease normally with increased car speed)
10b. Shift valve stuck (pressures appear normal)

11. No downshift
11a. Shift valve stuck
11b. Servo piston broken

12. No drive—forward or reverse
12a. Mechanical failure (line pressure is normal)
12b. Mechanical failure in or ahead of pump (no line pressure)
12c. Pressure regulator valve stuck (no line pressure)
12d. Extremely low oil level

13. Slipping
13a. Low oil level
13b. Failure of modulator bellows (line pressure does not increase with decrease in engine vacuum and upshifts occur extremely early)

13c. Pressure regulator valve stuck (low line pressure)

13d. Modulator valve stuck (low line pressure)

13e. Low band adjustment (slips in forward, normal in reverse)

14. Car creeps in NEUTRAL

14a. Forward clutch or low band not released

15. No drive in REVERSE

15a. Reverse clutch piston stuck

15b. Reverse clutch plates worn

15c. Reverse clutch seal leaking excessively

15d. Blocked reverse clutch apply orifice

16. Transmission case and extension oil seal leaks

16a. Extension oil seal defective

16b. Outer shift lever oil seal defective

16c. Speedometer driven gear fitting loose

16d. Oil cooler pipe connections loose

16e. Vacuum modulator assembly and case leaking

17. Oil forced out of filler tube

17a. Oil level too high, foaming caused by planet carrier running in oil

17b. Water in oil

17c. Leak in pump suction circuits

TROUBLESHOOTING A SUPER TURBINE 400 AUTOMATIC TRANSMISSION

APPLICATION: Buick and Cadillac, since 1964

Accurate diagnosis of apparent transmission problems begins with a thorough understanding of normal transmission operation; in particular, knowing which units are involved in the various speeds or shifts so that the specific units or circuits involved in the problem can be isolated and investigated further. Determine that all shifts are being obtained in the following manner:

THIRD–SECOND CHECK

Position the selector lever in the DRIVE position, and keep the car speed at approximately 35 mph. While gradually accelerating, move the selector lever to LO range. The transmission should downshift to second. An increase in engine rpm and an engine braking should be noticed.

SECOND–FIRST CHECK

Leave the selector lever in LO range and coast down to approximately 18 mph. The transmission should downshift to first gear. An increase in engine rpm and braking effect should be noted. The following sequence provides the desired information quickly and in most cases corrects the malfunction without requiring the removal of the transmission. It must be accomplished in the following sequence:

DIAGNOSIS SEQUENCE

A. Oil level

B. Oil pressure

C. Manual linkage

D. Engine idle and dash pot adjustment

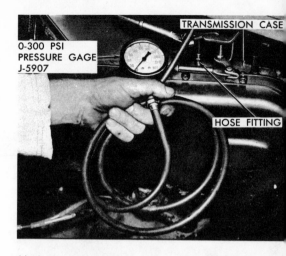

Method of connecting a pressure gauge to the Supe Turbine 400 automatic transmission.

E. Vacuum line

F. Vacuum modulator assembly

G. Detent switch and solenoid

H. Governor assembly

I. Control valve assembly

J. Rear servo assembly

K. Front servo assembly

L. Forward clutch

M. Intermediate clutch

N. Direct clutch

O. Front and rear bands

A. OIL LEVEL

Before attempting to check and/or correct any transmission complaint it is absolutely essential that the oil level be checked and corrected, if necessary. Either too high or too low an oil level can cause slippage in all ranges or excessive noise.

The oil level should be checked with the selector lever in the Park position, engine running, and the vehicle on a level pavement. The transmission oil should be at the operating temperature of 170° (This can be accomplished by driving approximately 5 miles with frequent starts and stops.) If the oil level is low, add automatic transmission fluid to the Full mark.

B. OIL PRESSURE

Check and correct the oil level. Before road testing an oil pressure gauge should be connected and the pressures checked as follows:

Engine idle pressure check. With the selector lever in DRIVE range and the vehicle running at 30 mph, with the throttle closed, the line pressure should be 70 psi.

Full throttle pressure check. A satisfactory full-throttle pressure check can be made with the acuum line removed from the carburetor, transmission in NEUTRAL, and engine speed at fast idle (700–1000 rpm). The pressure should be 145 psi.

In order to diagnose a specific shift trouble it may be necessary to check the line pressure at the full-throttle first-to-second and second-to-third shift points. If this becomes necessary, a road test must be made. The pressure at the first-to-second full-throttle shift point is 120 psi, and at the second-to-third full-throttle shift point, it is 100 psi. This check will point out any errors in the governor feed oil to the modulator.

If the pressure was low, check: (a) the vacuum modulator assembly for a loose attaching bolt, collapsed bellows, stuck modulator valve; (b) the pressure regulator valve and spring for sticking, plugged orifice, or a collapsed spring; and (c) the boost valve for sticking.

If the engine idle pressure was high, check: (a) the vacuum line, (b) the vacuum modulator for leaks, (c) the modulator valve for sticking, (d) the pressure regulator valve for sticking, and (e) the boost valve for sticking.

C. MANUAL LINKAGE

The safety switch should be adjusted so that the engine will start only in PARK or NEUTRAL. With the selector lever in PARK position, the parking pawl should prevent the vehicle from rolling. The pointer on the indicator quadrant should line up properly with the indicators in all ranges.

D. ENGINE IDLE SPEED AND DASH POT ADJUSTMENT

Adjust the idle speed and the dash pot to specifications given in the Appendix.

E. VACUUM LINE CHECK

Check the vacuum line for leaks, plugged, crimped, or a plugged carburetor orifice.

F. VACUUM MODULATOR ASSEMBLY

The vacuum modulator assembly controls the transmission line pressure. A faulty vacuum modulator assembly, such as a leaking diaphragm, bellows, or a stuck modulator valve may cause: (a) high line pressure, (b) low line pressure, (c) high shift points, (d) low shift points, (e) harsh shifts, (f) slipping shifts.

G. DETENT SWITCH AND SOLENOID

The detent switch and solenoid can be checked by listening for the detent solenoid to click while operating the switch by hand (with the ignition switch ON but the engine not running). If the solenoid did not engage, check the detent switch and adjust or replace the detent solenoid.

If the solenoid did engage, but the shift points were late (detent shifts), check for loose solenoid attaching screws, a mispositioned solenoid

gasket, the solenoid for a plugged orifice, for a leak between the control valve assembly spacer plate and the case, a bent spacer, a blown gasket, or the case face not flat.

H. GOVERNOR ASSEMBLY

The governor assembly controls the transmission shift points. A stuck governor can cause: (a) no upshift, (b) second or third gear start, (c) low or high line pressures.

I. CONTROL VALVE ASSEMBLY CHECK

The control valve assembly check involves a disassembly and a thorough inspection of the control valve assembly with attention to the following items: (a) The attaching bolts must not be loose or excessive leakage will occur between the adjacent channels. Over-torquing the bolts can cause distortion or warpage, which also causes leakage and sticking valves. (b) Distorted or mispositioned springs in the valve body. The position and condition of the springs is very important. (c) The valves should be free enough to fall because of their own weight. Burrs or small dents can be removed using a fine abrasive stone. The sharp edges on the valve lands should not be removed. (d) Porosity between channels or passages can be detected by using a solvent and observing if any leakage occurs. (e) The valve body, case, and spacer plate must be flat or cross leakage can occur. A surface plate and bluing is useful in checking for warpage of the bodies. Gentle and careful lapping of the valve body sealing faces will often correct a warped condition. (f) The rear servo applies the rear band in REVERSE and LO range first gear. It also is the accumulator for the first-to-second shift. A faulty rear servo, such as a leaking accumulator, or leaking servo piston oil seal, a stuck piston, or wrong piston pin, can cause: (1) slipping first-to-second shift, (2) harsh first-to-second shift, (3) slipping reverse, (4) no reverse, (5) no overrun braking in LO range.

K. FRONT SERVO

The front servo applies the front band in second gear for overrun braking. It also acts as an accumulator for the second-to-third shift. A faulty servo, such as a broken oil seal ring or stuck piston may cause: (a) slipping first-to-second shift, (b) slipping second-to-third shift, (c) no third gear, (d) no engine braking in second, or (e) harsh second-to-third shift.

L. FORWARD CLUTCH

The forward clutch is the connection between the converter and the transmission gear set and is applied in all forward driving ranges. No forward drive or a slipping first gear may be caused by the following: (a) missing or broken pump oil seal ring, (b) leaking inner or outer piston seal, (c) stuck check ball, or (d) worn clutch plates.

M. Intermediate Clutch

The intermediate clutch is applied in second gear, which makes the sprag effective in holding the sun gear shaft and sun gear from turning counterclockwise. A slipping first-to-second shift or no second gear may be caused by: (a) leaking piston seals, (b) worn clutch plates, or (c) loose case-to-center-support bolt.

N. Direct Clutch

The direct clutch is applied in third gear and reverse to drive the sun gear clockwise. A slipping second-to-third shift, slipping reverse, no third gear, or no reverse, may be caused by: (a) leaking piston seals, (b) stuck check ball, (c) broken or missing case support oil seal rings, (d) worn clutch plates, or (e) loose case-to-center support bolt.

O. Front and Rear Bands

The front and rear bands are used to back up the sprags for over-run braking. A broken or burnt front band will cause no second gear over-run braking. A broken or burnt rear band will cause no first gear over-run braking in LO range and no REVERSE.

DIAGNOSIS GUIDE

Condition	Possible Cause
No drive in DRIVE range	A-B-C-I-L
First speed only (no 1-2 shift)	F-G-H-I-J-M
No third gear (no 2-3 shift)	H-I-K-N
Drive in NEUTRAL	C-L
No reverse	A-B-C-I-J-N-O
Slipping—All ranges	A-B-F-H-I
Slipping—1-2 shift	A-B-F-I-J-K-M
Rough 1-2 shift	B-D-E-F-G-I-J-M
Slipping 2-3 shift	A-B-F-I-K-N
Rough 2-3 shift	B-D-E-F-G-I-N
No engine braking (Lo range second gear)	I-K-O
No engine braking (Lo range first gear)	I-J-O
No part-throttle downshifts	A-B-F-H-I
No detent downshifts	E-F-G-I
Low or high shift points	A-B-E-F-G-H-I

TROUBLESHOOTING THE REAR AXLE AND DRIVELINE

Due to the use of two driveshafts in many of today's cars, the driveline angles are very critical. Improper angles cause vibration and shudder.

There are two methods of checking the propeller shaft angles: one method uses an adapter which contains the built-in specified angle; the other uses a bubble-type protractor to compare the shaft angles with specifications.

In the first method (the adapter), the bubble is leveled against a boss on the rear end housing, the face of the companion flange, or the pan flange of the transmission. In the second method, the measured angles are compared with a horizontal line. In the second method, the car must be level to start with. The measurements can be taken with the car over a pit or supported on a hoist which lifts the car by the suspension system; a frame-contact hoist cannot be used.

Using the Adapter Method. Position the gauge against the right side of the transmission oil pan so that the contact surfaces seat properly. Adjust the leveling screw until the bubble is centered.

To measure the propeller shaft angle, position the gauge against the front propeller shaft so that

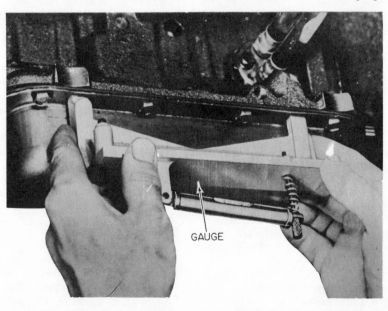

GAUGE

To set the protractor to the angle of the engine, a special adapter is placed against the transmission oil pan and then adjusted to center the bubble.

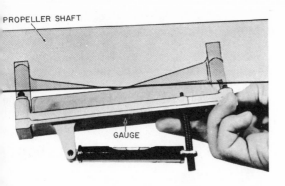

PROPELLER SHAFT

GAUGE

To measure the angle of the driveshaft, the adapter positioned as shown. The angle of the shaft is orrect when the bubble is centered.

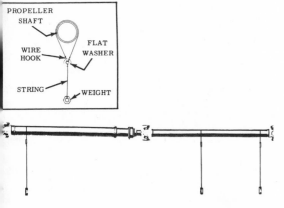

PROPELLER SHAFT

WIRE HOOK

FLAT WASHER

STRING

WEIGHT

For lateral alignment with two shafts and three universal joints, hang three weighted strings as shown. ight along the strings for alignment. Shift the center niversal joint support until the strings line up.

the contact surfaces of the gauge seat squarely against the shaft. The bubble should be within $\frac{1}{16}''$ from the center. If it is not, shims must be added or removed from the center support until the angle is correct.

Using the Protractor Method. Place the protractor against the back side of the rear axle pinion flange in a vertical position. Adjust the spirit level until the bubble is centered. Record the number of degrees that the pinion flange tips down from a true vertical position.

Now, place the protractor against the propeller shaft and adjust the spirit level until the bubble is centered. This will show the number of degrees that the propeller shaft tips up toward the front of the car from a horizontal position.

Add the number of degrees the rear pinion flange is away from the true vertical to the number of degrees the propeller shaft is away from the true horizontal. The total of these two will give the working angle of the rear universal joint, which for Chrysler products should be between 1° and 3°.

TROUBLESHOOTING THE REAR AXLE

A rear axle should not be disassembled until a thorough diagnosis is made of the trouble and symptoms observed during the operation of the car. The most common rear axle complaint is noise. Care must be taken to be sure that the noise is not caused by the engine, tires, transmission, wheel bearings, or some other part of the car.

Before road testing the car, make sure sufficient lubricant is in the axle housing and inflate the tires to the correct pressure. Drive the car far enough to warm the lubricant to its normal operating temperature before making the tests.

Engine noise or exhaust noise can be detected by parking the car and running the engine at various

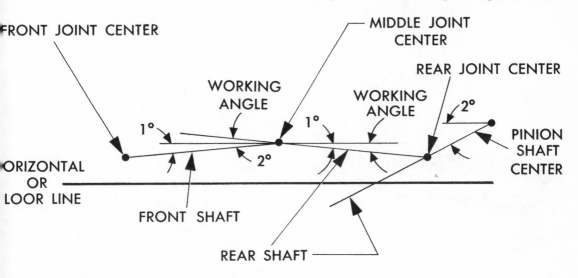

FRONT JOINT CENTER

MIDDLE JOINT CENTER

REAR JOINT CENTER

WORKING ANGLE

1°

WORKING ANGLE

1°

2°

PINION SHAFT CENTER

ORIZONTAL OR LOOR LINE

2°

FRONT SHAFT

REAR SHAFT

The universal joint working angle of Chrysler products is 2°.

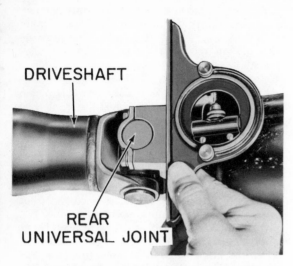

DRIVESHAFT

REAR
UNIVERSAL JOINT

To measure the angle of the rear axle, the protractor is positioned against the back side of the flange
as shown.

speeds with the transmission in neutral. A portable
tachometer will assist in duplicating road speeds
at which the noises occurred.

Tire noise can be detected by driving the car
over various road surfaces. Tire noise is minimized
on smooth asphalt or black-top roads. Switching
tires can help to detect or eliminate tire noises.

Wheel bearing noise can sometimes be detected
by jacking up each wheel in turn and feeling for
roughness as the wheel is rotated. Wheel bearing
noise is most obvious on a low-speed coast. Applying the brakes lightly while the car is moving will
often reduce or eliminate the noise caused by a
defective wheel bearing.

A car should be tested for axle and driveline
noise by operating it under four driving conditions:

1. Drive: Higher than normal road-load power,
where the speed gradually increases on level road
acceleration.

2. Cruise: Constant speed operation at normal
road speeds.

3. Float: Using only enough throttle to keep the
car from driving the engine. Car will slow down
(very little load on rear axle gears).

Then the propeller shaft angle is determined by
placing the protractor as shown.

4. Coast: Throttle closed—engine is braking the
car (load is on the coast side of the gear set).

Backlash or play in the running gear can be
checked by driving the car on a smooth road at
25 mph and lightly pressing and releasing the accelerator pedal. Backlash is indicated by a slapping
noise with each movement of the accelerator pedal.
Raising the car on a lubrication rack will permit
you to make a more detailed examination.

REAR AXLE TROUBLESHOOTING CHART

TROUBLES & CAUSES

1. **Noise on acceleration**
   1a. Heavy heel contact on ring gear
2. **Noise on coast**
   2a. Heavy toe contact on ring gear
3. **Noise on both coast and acceleration**
   3a. Differential gears worn
   3b. Pinion and ring gears worn
   3c. Defective bearings
4. **Noise only when rounding a curve**
   4a. Damaged differential case gears
5. **Backlash**
   5a. Worn axle shaft splines
   5b. Loose axle shaft nut
   5c. Worn universal joints
   5d. Excessive play between pinion and ring gear
   5e. Worn differential bearings
   5f. Worn differential side gear thrust washers
   and/or case
6. **Vibration**
   6a. Worn universal joints
   6b. Universal spline not assembled according to
   matching arrows
   6c. Undercoating applied to drive shaft
   6d. Drive line center bearing out of alignment
   6e. Drive line angle incorrect

SURE-GRIP DIFFERENTIAL TROUBLE-
SHOOTING CHART

APPLICATION: Optional equipment on all cars

TROUBLES & CAUSES

1. **Noises, other than differential**
   Rear axle noises are often confused with sounds
   that originate in other parts of the car; such as
   wheel bearings, loose wheel bolts, tires, clutch,
   transmission, and universal joints. Always make
   a careful inspection of these units before con-
   demning the rear axle.
   1a. Tires: Tire noise will vary, depending on the
   type of road surface and the condition of the
   tire treads. Road testing on different pave-
   ments will usually indicate whether or not the
   tires are the cause of the noise.
   1b. Wheel bearings: To determine if the wheel
   bearings are causing the noise, road test the
   car and apply the brakes. This action will take
   some of the load off the wheel bearings. If
   the noise diminishes, the bearings may be at
   fault.
   1c. Exhaust: Test for exhaust system noise by
   slowing and increasing engine speed with the

car standing still. Noise should be apparent as long as the engine speed is steady. But it will fade when the engine speed is changed. Loose tail pipe brackets or a bent tail pipe will cause a rattling noise.

1d. Clutch: Noise resulting from a faulty clutch disc may be heard when the car is accelerating between 25–30 mph, or while coasting down from 45–38 mph.

1e. Propeller shaft: An unbalanced shaft can cause excessive vibration and noise at speeds above 50 mph.

1f. Axle shaft: Excessive end play in the rear axle shafts will cause a thump or chuckling noise when driving on a rough road, or when turning a corner.

2. **Noises in the differential and carrier assembly**

The main difference between an axle bearing noise and a gear noise is in the duration and the sound. Bearing noise is continuous and may change in volume only as the speed changes. Slightly worn or damaged bearings cause a "sizzling" noise. Badly worn or broken bearings will make a rough grating sound. A continuous whine may be produced by a pinion and ring gear that are set up too tightly. Gear noise comes in when the car is being driven under load, on the coast, or on both the pull and coast. But gear noises change in volume and pitch as the car speed changes. There may also be a combination of bearing and gear noises.

2a. Steady noise on pull: Loss of lubricant, the use of an improper lubricant, or the improper mesh of the gears will cause a steady hum.

2b. Steady noise on coast: Gear teeth that are badly scored due to excessive end play in the pinion bearings, or because of improper adjustment of the bearings, will cause a steady hum.

2c. Bearing noise on pull and coast: When the pinion or differential bearings are scored, chipped, cracked, or badly worn, a noise will be heard when accelerating or coasting down.

2d. Ring gear and pinion: A sharp, metallic sound, heard when shifting from reverse to a forward speed, indicates that the ring gear may be creeping on the case or that the mounting bolts are loose. It may also be caused by a loose axle shaft nut. A thumping sound, heard when the car is turning a corner, may be due to a broken tooth, or a large nick in a differential side gear.

3. **Leakage**

3a. If the vent is plugged, leakage of the rear axle lubricant may result.

3b. If there is an excessive amount of lubricant in the differential, high pressure will build up and force the lubricant out through the seals and gasket.

TROUBLESHOOTING THE FRONT END

Drive the car on a smooth road at about 30 mph, and then take your hands off the steering wheel. The car should maintain a straight course. If the road is crowned, it may cause the car to wander toward the low side of the road and, therefore, it may be necessary to make this test evenly straddled over the center line. Choose a road with no traffic to make this test. On a windy day, the test should be duplicated by going back and forth over the same road. Uneven front-end angles will cause the car to wander to one side.

Hold your hand lightly on the steering wheel at about 30 mph to check whether any shocks are being transmitted back to the steering wheel. A constantly jiggling wheel indicates that the front wheels are out of balance. This constant movement is very tiring to a driver on long trips and is hard on every moving part of the front end.

Turn into a deserted side street at about 25 mph, and then release the steering wheel; it should come back to a straight-ahead position without any assistance from the driver; otherwise, there is binding in the linkage, insufficient caster, or insufficient steering axis inclination.

To check for misalignment, stop the car and inspect the front tires for uneven tread wear. Pass your hand over the surface of each tire tread. Sharp edges felt going one way are called feather edges and are developed from sideward scuffing. Be especially critical of the right-front tire wear, as this wheel is most frequently knocked out of alignment by bumping the curb. When the right-front wheel tire is worn more unevenly than the left, it is an indication of a bent steering arm.

FRONT-END TROUBLESHOOTING CHART

TROUBLES & CAUSES

1. **Excessive looseness**
    1a. Improper adjustment of the steering gear
    1b. Worn steering linkage
    1c. Loose wheel bearing adjustment on worm bearings
    1d. Worn king pins or ball joints
    1e. Loose steering gear mounting
2. **Hard steering**
    2a. Tight adjustment of the steering gear
    2b. Lubrication needed
    2c. Low tire pressure
    2d. Wheels out of alignment
    2e. Excessive caster
3. **Wanders**
    3a. Loose front wheel bearings
    3b. Loose steering linkage
    3c. Loose front end supports
    3d. Uneven tire pressure
    3e. Low pressure in both rear tires
    3f. Incorrect caster
    3g. Bent spindle arm
    3h. Sagging spring
4. **Pulls to one side**
    4a. Uneven caster
    4b. Uneven camber
    4c. Uneven tire pressure
    4d. Frame out of alignment
    4e. Tire sizes not uniform
    4f. Bent spindle arm
    4g. Sagging spring

5. **Shimmy, low speed**
   5a. Loose support arms
   5b. Loose linkage
   5c. Loose wheel bearings
   5d. Soft springs
   5e. Static unbalance of front wheels
   5f. Incorrect tire pressure
6. **Shimmy, high speed**
   6a. Dynamic unbalance of front wheels
   6b. Too much caster
   6c. Soft springs
7. **Squeals on turns**
   7a. Low tire pressure
   7b. Incorrect camber
   7c. Bent spindle arm
   7d. Frame out of alignment
8. **Excessive tire wear**
   8a. Improper toe in
   8b. Improper turning radius
   8c. Underinflation
   8d. Overinflation
   8e. Grabbing
   8f. Excessive camber

TROUBLESHOOTING A POWER-STEERING UNIT

APPLICATION:

ROTARY-VALVE TYPE. Lincoln, and all General Motors cars except Chevrolet.

CONSTANT-CONTROL TYPE. All Chrysler products.

LINKAGE TYPE. Chevrolet, and all Ford products, except Lincoln.

Preliminary Checks. All conventional steering troubles apply and should be checked out first. Two tests apply to a power steering system: an oil pressure test and a turning-effort test.

Check the pump belt to see if it is worn or loose. If worn, replace it; if loose, adjust it. Check the fluid level; if low, add Automatic Transmission Fluid, Type A to bring the level to the full mark. Check the system for fluid leaks by running the engine and inspecting all joints where leakage could occur. Tighten all loose fittings and replace any damaged hoses. Check the turning effort by hooking a scale to the steering wheel. With the engine running, the car on a dry concrete floor, and the front tires properly inflated, the results should be as follows:

SPECIFICATION LIMITS

Type	Effort Required to Pull the Steering Wheel	Operating Pressure (psi)
Rotary-valve type	3½–5 lbs.	975–1,100
Constant-control type	20 ft. lbs. of torque	875–950
Linkage type	7–12 lbs.	800–1,000

Testing the Pressure of the System. Disconnect the pressure line at the oil pump. Attach a pressure gauge to the pump. With the engine warm and idling and the gauge valve open, note the oil pressure while turning the steering wheel from one extreme position to the other. Also note the maximum pressure built up with the wheel held in either the extreme right or left position. *CAUTION: Do not hold the wheel in an extreme position for an*

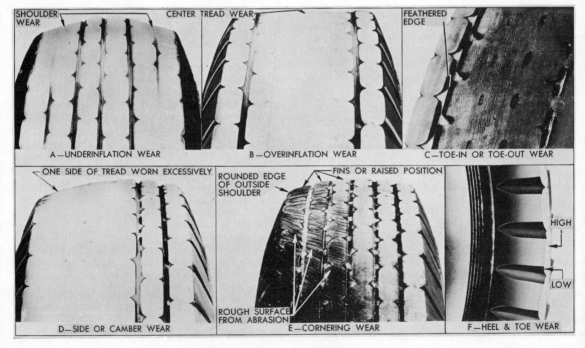

Types of tire wear and their causes.

Method of measuring the turning effort with a spring balance.

extended period because the oil temperature rises quickly, which can cause undue wear on the oil pump.

With the oil temperature between 150°F. and 170°F., as measured in the reservoir, the maximum oil pressure should not be less than 1000 psi. If the maximum pressure is less, it indicates trouble in the pump, oil hoses, steering gear, or a combination of these parts. To eliminate the hoses and gear, make a second test by closing the gauge valve and quickly testing the pressure of the pump alone, with the engine idling. Then open the valve to avoid an increase in oil temperature. A minimum pressure of 1000 psi should be present with the valve closed.

Comparing the maximum pressures obtained in the two tests will indicate the source of the trouble as follows: if the pressure is low in the first test and normal in the second, it indicates faulty external oil lines or steering gear. If the pressure is equally low in both tests, it indicates a faulty oil pump.

ROTARY-VALVE TYPE POWER STEERING TROUBLESHOOTING CHART

TROUBLES & CAUSES

1. **Hard steering while driving**
   1a. Lower coupling flange rubbing against the adjuster plug
   1b. Steering adjustment too tight
   1c. Insufficient pressure build-up in the power cylinder due to a leak or faulty valve
2. **Poor return of the steering wheel to center**
   2a. Lower coupling flange rubbing against the adjuster plug
   2b. Steering gear misalignment
   2c. Tight pitman sector-to-rack piston nut adjustment
   2d. Rack piston-to-worm preload too tight
   2e. Thrust bearing adjustment incorrect
   2f. Sticky valve spool
3. **Car leads to one side**
   3a. Badly worn valve

4. **Momentary increase in effort required when turning the wheel fast**
   4a. Air in system
   4b. Low oil level in the pump
   4c. High internal leakage
5. **Excessive wheel kickback or loose steering**
   5a. Air in system
   5b. Excessive lash between the pitman shaft sector and the rack piston
   5c. Loose thrust bearing adjustment
   5d. Rack piston nut-to-worm preload too low
6. **Steering wheel surges or jerks when turning with the engine running**
   6a. Loose pump belt
7. **Hard steering when parking**
   7a. Loose pump belt
   7b. Low oil level in reservoir
   7c. Steering gear adjustments too tight
   7d. Insufficient oil pressure
8. **No effort required to turn the steering wheel**
   8a. Broken torsion bar
9. **Gear noise (rattle or chuckle)**
   9a. Loose over-center adjustment. *NOTE: A slight rattle may occur on turns because of the increased lash off the high point. This is normal; therefore, it must not be reduced below the specified limits.*
   9b. Steering gear housing loose on frame
10. **Gear noise (hissing)**
    10a. A hissing noise is natural when the steering wheel is at the end of its travel, or when slowly turning the wheel with the car stationary. Do not replace the valve unless the hiss is objectionable.
    10b. The safety drive riveted pins may be making a metal-to-metal contact around the flexible coupling
11. **Pump noise**
    11a. Loose belt

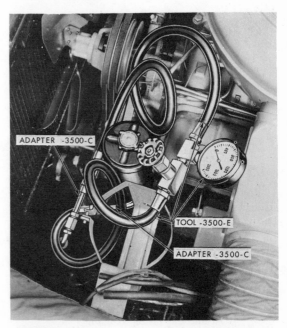

Method of hooking up a pressure gauge to test the operating pressures of a power steering system.

11b. Hoses touching parts of the car
11c. Low oil level
11d. Air in the oil
11e. Excessive back pressure caused by a restriction in a hose. With the engine running at 1500 rpm, the pressure between the pump and the gear should not exceed 125 psi with the steering wheel stationary
11f. Scored pressure plate
11g. Vanes not properly installed
11h. Vanes sticking in the rotor slots
11i. Extreme wear on pump ring
11j. Face of the thrust plate scored
11k. Scored rotor
11l. Defective flow plunger

12. Valve noise (squawk)
12a. Cut or worn dampener "O" ring on the valve spool
12b. Loose or worn valves

13. Defective oil pump
13a. Loose drive belt
13b. Low oil level
13c. Air in oil
13d. Defective hoses
13e. Flow control valve stuck open
13f. Loose screw in the end of the flow control valve
13g. Pressure plate not flat against the ring
13h. Worn pump ring
13i. Scored pressure plate, thrust plate, and/or rotor
13j. Vanes not properly installed
13k. Vanes sticking in rotor slots
13l. Faulty flow control valve assembly

CONSTANT CONTROL POWER STEERING TROUBLESHOOTING CHART

TROUBLES & CAUSES

1. Hard steering
1a. Tires not properly inflated
1b. Low oil level (usually accompanied by pump noises)
1c. Loose pump belt
1d. Oil on pump belt
1e. Steering linkage needs lubrication
1f. Power steering pump output low
1g. Steering gear malfunctions:
  (1) Cross shaft adjustment too tight
  (2) Pressure control valve stuck in closed position
  (3) External oil leakage at the following points: lower sector shaft oil seal, sector shaft adjusting screw seal, sector shaft cover "O" ring seal, and valve housing-to-gear housing "O" rings
  (4) Defective or damaged valve lever. If the pressure gauge will build up to 850–950 psi, check the following points: defective or damaged gear shaft bearings; dirt or chips in the steering gear; damaged column support worm shaft bearings; damaged thrust bearing or excessive preload adjustment; or a rough, hard-to-turn worm and piston assembly
  (5) Excessive internal leakage. If the pressure gauge will not build up to 850–950 psi,

check the following points: cylinder head "O" rings; cylinder head reaction seal; cylinder head worm shaft oil seal assembly; column support-to-ferrule "O" ring seal; column support reaction seal; and the cylinder head "O" rings

2. Poor recovery from turns
2a. Tires not properly inflated
2b. Steering linkage binding
2c. Improper wheel alignment
2d. Damaged or defective steering tube bearing
2e. Steering wheel column jacket and steering unit not properly aligned
2f. Steering gear malfunctions:
  (1) Improper cross shaft mesh adjustment
  (2) Pressure control valve piston stuck in *open* position
  (3) Column support spanner nut loose
  (4) Defective or damaged valve lever
  (5) Improper worm thrust bearing adjustment
  (6) Burrs or nicks in reaction ring grooves in cylinder head
  (7) Defective or damaged cylinder head worm shaft seal ring
  (8) Dirt or chips in steering gear unit
  (9) Rough or catchy worm and piston assembly

3. Temporary increase in effort when turning steering
3a. Low oil level
3b. Loose pump belt
3c. Oil on pump belt
3d. Binding steering linkage
3e. Engine idled too slow
3f. Defective power steering pump
3g. Air in system. (Work steering wheel from right to left until air is expelled.)
3h. Gear malfunctions:
  (1) External leakage
  (2) Improper cross shaft adjustment
  (3) Excessive internal leakage

4. Excessive steering wheel free play
4a. Improper cross shaft adjustment
4b. Column support spanner nut loose
4c. Improper worm thrust bearing adjustment

5. Lack of assistance—one direction
5a. Oil leaking past worm shaft cast iron oil seal ring or ferrule "O" ring

6. Lack of assistance—both directions
6a. Broken "D" ring on worm piston
6b. Piston end plug loose
6c. Reaction seal missing
6d. Pump belt slipping
6e. Pump output low

7. Noises
7a. Buzzing noise in neutral, stops when steering wheel is turned—sticking pressure control valve
7b. Noisy power pump
7c. Damaged hydraulic lines
7d. Pressure control valve sticking
7e. Improper sector shaft mesh adjustment
7f. Air in system

8. Self-steering—or leads to one side
8a. Tires not properly inflated
8b. Improper wheel alignment
8c. Steering wheel off-center when car is traveling straight ahead

8d. Valve body out of adjustment:
   (1) Steering to the left—move steering valve housing *down* on steering housing
   (2) Steering to the right—move steering valve housing *up* on steering housing
8e. Valve lever damaged
8f. Column support spanner nut loose

LINKAGE-TYPE POWER STEERING TROUBLESHOOTING CHART

TROUBLES & CAUSES

1. **Binding or poor recovery**
   1a. Steering gear shaft binding
   1b. Steering gear out of adjustment
   1c. Steering linkage binding
   1d. Valve spool binding due to dirt or burred edges
   1e. Valve spool out of adjustment
   1f. Interference at sector shaft arm and ball stud
   1g. Travel regulator stop out of adjustment
   1h. Valve sleeve damaged
2. **Hard steering**
   2a. Pump belt out of adjustment
   2b. Pump output low
   2c. Air in system
   2d. Steering gear out of adjustment
   2e. Valve spool out of adjustment
   2f. Valve spool sticking
   2g. Steering linkage binding
3. **Loss of power assist**
   3a. Pump inoperative
   3b. Lines damaged
   3c. Power cylinder damaged
   3d. Valve spool out of adjustment
4. **Loss of power assist—one direction**
   4a. Valve spool out of adjustment
   4b. By-pass valve in control valve inoperative
5. **Looseness in steering**
   5a. Steering gear out of adjustment
   5b. Steering linkage worn
   5c. Valve spool out of adjustment
   5d. Valve spool centering spring defective
6. **Noisy pump**
   6a. Air being drawn into pump
   6b. Lines touching other parts of car
   6c. Oil level low
   6d. Excessive back pressure caused by obstructions in lines
   6e. Excessive wear of internal parts
   6f. Vanes sticking

TROUBLESHOOTING A CONVENTIONAL HYDRAULIC BRAKE SYSTEM

Perhaps the most common complaint about brakes is that the car cannot be brought to a satisfactory stop. As the lining wears, the brake pedal must be pushed down farther and farther in order to move the brake shoes into contact with the drums. Eventually, it reaches the floorboard, and an emergency application does not stop the car. When this happens, it is necessary to adjust the position of the brake shoes so that they are closer to the drums. This restores the pedal to its former position.

Generally, a soft pedal, or one that goes slowly to the floorboard under continued pressure, is caused by air trapped in the hydraulic lines or to a leak in the system. The system must be bled to get rid of the air. To repair the leak, the defective unit must be removed. However, it is considered good practice to overhaul the entire hydraulic system in the event of a leak in any one part, because all of the units are in the same condition; unless repaired at the same time, they too will soon leak.

Another frequent complaint has to do with noise. Actually, the squeals and squeaks that are heard are due to loose parts, which cause high-frequency vibration.

CONVENTIONAL HYDRAULIC BRAKE SYSTEM TROUBLESHOOTING CHART

TROUBLES & CAUSES

1. **Pedal goes to floorboard**
   1a. Brake shoes out of adjustment
   1b. Brake fluid level low
   1c. Leaking lines or cylinders
   1d. Air in brake lines
   1e. Defective master cylinder
2. **One brake drags**
   2a. Incorrect shoe adjustment
   2b. Clogged brake line
   2c. Sluggish wheel cylinder piston
   2d. Weak brake shoe return spring
   2e. Loose wheel bearing
   2f. Brake shoe binding on backing plate
   2g. Out-of-round drum
3. **All brakes drag**
   3a. Insufficient play in master cylinder push rod
   3b. Master cylinder relief port plugged
   3c. Lubricating oil in system instead of hydraulic fluid
   3d. Master cylinder piston sticking
4. **Car pulls to one side**
   4a. Brake fluid or grease on lining
   4b. Sluggish wheel cylinder piston
   4c. Weak retracting spring
   4d. Loose wheel bearing
   4e. Wrong brake lining
   4f. Drum out-of-round
5. **Soft pedal**
   5a. Air in system
   5b. Improper anchor adjustment
   5c. Improper linings
   5d. Thin drums
   5e. Warped brake shoes
6. **Hard pedal**
   6a. Wrong brake lining
   6b. Glazed brake lining
   6c. Mechanical resistance at pedal or shoes
7. **One or more wheels grab**
   7a. Grease or hydraulic fluid on lining
   7b. Loose wheel bearings
   7c. Loose front end supports
   7d. Loose backing plate
   7e. Distorted brake shoe
   7f. Improper brake lining
   7g. Primary and secondary shoes reversed
8. **Erratic braking action**
   8a. Loose brake support

8b. Loose front end suspension parts
8c. Grease or hydraulic fluid on lining
8d. Binding of the shoes in the guides
8e. Sticking hydraulic wheel cylinder piston

9. Noisy brakes
9a. Loose backing plate
9b. Loose wheel bearing adjustment
9c. Loose front end supports
9d. Warped brake shoes
9e. Linings loose on shoes
9f. Improperly installed brake shoes
9g. Improper anchor adjustment
9h. Loose brake shoe guides
9i. Weak brake return springs
9j. Dust in rivet holes
9k. Grease or hydraulic fluid on brake lining

TROUBLESHOOTING THE CALIPER DISC BRAKE SYSTEM

Disc brakes are mounted on the front wheels and non-servo, single-anchor, self-adjusting, internal-expanding, drum-type brakes are used on the rear; except for Corvette, which has disc brakes on all four wheels. The brakes are powered by a vacuum-suspended type booster unit. Ford products have a proportioning valve in the brake lines between the master cylinder and rear wheel cylinders. The Lincoln disc brake system has an additional metering valve between the master cylinder and the front wheel disc brakes to limit action until a predetermined pressure is reached.

The usual hydraulic brake troubleshooting procedures apply, with the following troubles applying especially to the disc brake system:

CALIPER　　　　　　DISC

Mounting position of a caliper disc brake assembly.

CALIPER DISC BRAKE TROUBLE-SHOOTING CHART

TROUBLES & CAUSES

1. Excessive pedal travel
1a. Friction pad knock-back after violent cornering
1b. Friction pads not properly seated or positioned
1c. Insufficient fluid in master cylinder reservoir
1d. Loose wheel bearing adjustment
1e. Damaged caliper piston seal
1f. Improper booster push rod adjustment

2. Brake roughness or pedal chatter
2a. Excessive lateral runout of disc
2b. Sides of disc not parallel

3. Excessive pedal effort
3a. Pistons seized
3b. Brake fluid or grease on lining
3c. Friction pads worn beyond specifications
3d. Proportioning valve malfunction (Ford products only)
3e. Inoperative booster unit

4. Pulls to one side
4a. Piston(s) seized
4b. Brake fluid or grease on lining
4c. Caliper not in alignment with disc
4d. Loose caliper

5. Groan
5a. Normal under certain conditions of pedal pressure

6. Rattle
6a. Excessive clearance between caliper and friction pad
6b. Friction pad hold-down clips missing or improperly positioned

7. Brakes heat up and fail to release
7a. Seized piston(s)
7b. Driver rides brake pedal

8. Leaky wheel cylinder
8a. Damaged piston seal
8b. Scored bores
8c. Corroded bores and/or piston

9. Grabbing or uneven braking action
9a. Seized piston(s)
9b. Brake fluid or grease on friction pads
9c. Proportioning valve malfunction (Ford products only)
9d. Caliper out of alignment with disc
9e. Caliper loose on bracket

10. No braking effort when pedal is depressed
10a. Friction pad(s) not properly seated or positioned
10b. Insufficient fluid in system
10c. Damaged piston seal
10d. Bleeder screw open

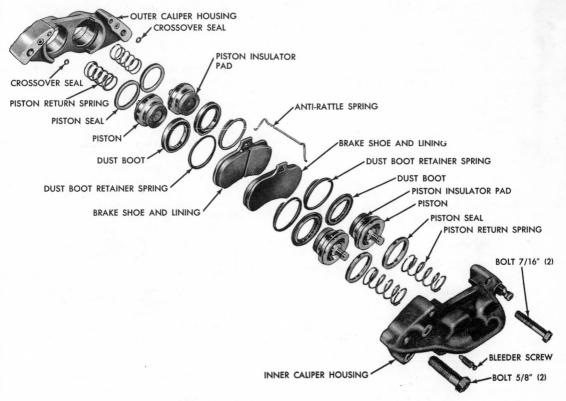

OUTER CALIPER HOUSING
CROSSOVER SEAL
PISTON INSULATOR PAD
CROSSOVER SEAL
PISTON RETURN SPRING
PISTON SEAL
PISTON
DUST BOOT
DUST BOOT RETAINER SPRING
BRAKE SHOE AND LINING
ANTI-RATTLE SPRING
BRAKE SHOE AND LINING
DUST BOOT RETAINER SPRING
DUST BOOT
PISTON INSULATOR PAD
PISTON
PISTON SEAL
PISTON RETURN SPRING
BOLT 7/16" (2)
BLEEDER SCREW
INNER CALIPER HOUSING
BOLT 5/8" (2)

Exploded view of the Chrysler disc brake assembly.

TROUBLESHOOTING A POWER BRAKE SYSTEM

APPLICATION:

COMBINED-UNIT TYPE. All cars except Ford and Chrysler products.

BOOSTER-TYPE. Ford and all Chrysler products.

Preliminary Checks. All of the conventional brake-system troubles apply to a power brake system and they should be checked out first. To isolate power brake trouble, proceed as follows:

Road test the car and make a brake application at about 20 mph to determine whether the vehicle stops evenly and quickly. If the pedal has a spongy feel when applying the brakes, air is present in the hydraulic system.

With the engine stopped and the transmission in neutral, apply the brakes several times to deplete all vacuum reserve in the system. Depress the brake pedal, hold a light foot pressure on the pedal, and start the engine. If the vacuum system is operating, the pedal will tend to fall away under foot pressure, and less pressure will be required to hold the pedal in an applied position. If no action is felt, the vacuum system is not functioning. Stop the engine and again deplete all vacuum reserve in the system. Depress the brake pedal

and hold foot pressure on the pedal. If the pedal gradually falls away under foot pressure, the hydraulic system is leaking.

Start the engine. With the brakes off, run the engine to a medium speed and turn off the ignition, immediately closing the throttle. This builds up vacuum. Wait 90 sec. and then try the brake action. If there is no vacuum assist for three or more applications, the vacuum check valve is faulty.

If the brake pedal travels to within 1" of the floorboard, the brakes require adjustment or the brake shoes require relining.

COMBINED-UNIT TYPE POWER BRAKE TROUBLESHOOTING CHART

TROUBLES & CAUSES

1. **Hard pedal**
   1a. Faulty vacuum check valve
   1b. Collapsed vacuum hose
   1c. Plugged or loose vacuum fittings, hose, or pipes
   1d. Vacuum leak between vacuum power cylinder and hydraulic master cylinder
   1e. Leak in vacuum reservoir tank
   1f. Bound-up pedal mechanism
   1g. Internal vacuum hose loose or restricted
   1h. Jammed air valve

1i. Vacuum leaks in unit caused by loose piston plate screws, loose piston packing, leaks between hydraulic master cylinder and vacuum power cylinder, or by a faulty master cylinder piston or vacuum seal

1j. Defective diaphragm

1k. Restricted air cleaner

2. **Grabby brakes (off-and-on condition)**
   2a. Sticking air valve
   2b. Master cylinder piston binding in power piston guide
   2c. Dented or distorted power cylinder housing

3. **Pedal goes to floorboard**
   3a. Brake out of adjustment
   3b. Fluid reservoir needs replenishing
   3c. Defective primary or secondary cup
   3d. Defective head nut or head nut gasket
   3e. Cracked master cylinder casting
   3f. Leaks at wheel cylinder, in pipes, or in connections
   3g. Defective annular ring on cylinder plug
   3h. Faulty master cylinder check valve that has permitted air to enter system, causing a spongy pedal

4. **Brakes fail to release**
   4a. Faulty check valve at head nut
   4b. Excessive friction at seal of the master cylinder piston
   4c. Excessive friction at power piston cup
   4d. Blocked air passage in power piston
   4e. Air cleaner blocked or choked
   4f. Air valve sticking shut
   4g. Broken piston return spring
   4h. Broken air valve spring

BOOSTER-TYPE POWER BRAKE TROUBLESHOOTING CHART

TROUBLES & CAUSES

1. **Hard pedal**
   1a. No vacuum to booster unit
   1b. Incorrect adjustment of valve-adjusting eccentric
   1c. Bent pedal trigger

2. **Pedal chatters**
   2a. Incorrect adjustment of valve-adjusting eccentric
   2b. Incorrect adjustment of master cylinder push rod

3. **Slow pedal return**
   3a. Clogged air filter
   3b. Incorrect master cylinder push rod adjustment

AIR-CONDITIONING TROUBLESHOOTING CHART

TROUBLES & CAUSES

1. **Drafts**
   1a. Poor air outlet adjustment
   1b. Car temperature too low due to a stuck thermostat switch

2. **Shortage of air supply at outlets**
   2a. Car temperature up due to improper position of controls, slipping fan, or clogged air passage through the cooling coil
   2b. Low fan speed due to low voltage or bad bearings

3. **Water dripping into passenger compartment**
   3a. Drip pan or drain tubes stopped up
   3b. Housing sweating

4. **Hissing noise at expansion valve**
   4a. Shortage of refrigerant. Check the sight glass
   4b. Restriction in the liquid line

5. **Partial frosting and sweating of the cooling unit or poor cooling**
   5a. Improperly adjusted controls
   5b. Heater valve does not cut off circulation of the engine coolant through the heater core with the heat control *off*
   5c. Shortage of refrigerant
   5d. Restricted or clogged liquid line
   5e. Thermostat switch inoperative
   5f. Expansion valve inoperative

6. **Failure to cool**
   6a. Heater valve does not cut off circulation of the engine coolant through the heater core with the HEAT control in the *off* position
   6b. Faulty thermostat switch
   6c. Slipping clutch
   6d. Loss of refrigerant charge
   6e. Blower not operating properly
   6f. Insufficient air
   6g. Stopped up liquid line or receiver-dehydrator
   6h. Faulty expansion valve

7. **Intermittent failure to cool**
   7a. Freeze-up in high humidity areas which can be corrected by raising the low limit of the thermostat switch

8. **Too cool**
   8a. Faulty thermostat switch
   8b. Stuck clutch

9. **High gauge reading on the high side of the system**
   9a. Air or excessive refrigerant in the system
   9b. Blocked air circulation through the condenser
   9c. High engine temperature

10. **Low gauge reading on the high side of the system**
    10a. Shortage of refrigerant
    10b. Faulty compressor

11. **High gauge reading on the low side of the system**
    11a. Clutch slippage
    11b. Excessively high head or side pressure
    11c. Over-feeding of the expansion valve
    11d. Faulty compressor

12. **Low gauge reading on the low side of the system**
    12a. Shortage of refrigerant
    12b. Clutch will not disengage
    12c. Restriction in the liquid line, suction line, receiver-dehydrator, or screen at the expansion valve
    12d. Cooling coil dirty or iced up